DATE DUE			

Twayne's Filmmakers Series

Warren French
EDITOR

Chaplin

This formal portrait of Chaplin has been chosen for the frontispiece because it is the only photograph of himself Chaplin displays in a film—it hangs over Calvero's mantle in Limelight.

Chaplin

JULIAN SMITH

BOSTON

Twayne Publishers

1984

Chaplin

is first published in 1984 by Twayne Publishers,
A Division of G. K. Hall & Company
All Rights Reserved

Copyright © 1984 by G. K. Hall & Company

Book Production by John Amburg

Printed on permanent/durable acid-free paper and bound
in the United States of America.

First Paperback Edition, August 1984

Production Stills courtesy of the Museum of
Modern Art/Film Stills Archive.

Library of Congress Cataloging in Publication Data

Smith, Julian, 1937–
Chaplin.

(Twayne's filmmakers series)
Bibliography: p. 152
Filmography: p. 154
Includes Index.
1. Chaplin, Charlie, 1889–1977.   2. Comedians—United
States—Biography.   3. Moving-picture producers and
directors—United States—Biography.   I. Title.
II. Series

PN2287.C5S56   1984   791.43′028′0924   [B]   83-22772
ISBN 0-8057-9294-5
ISBN 0-8057-9302-X (pbk.)

for
Samuel Kipnis
in gratitude for his generosity to
the Film Studies Program
at the University of Florida

Contents

About the Author

JULIAN SMITH studied at Tulane and Columbia, where he was a Woodrow Wilson Fellow. He has taught at Georgetown, the University of New Hampshire, Ithaca College, San Diego State University, and the University of Florida, where he teaches in the Film Studies Program.

In addition to many articles in the popular press and about forty scholarly or critical essays in academic journals, he has published *Looking Away: Hollywood and Vietnam* and *Nevil Shute* (in the Twayne English Authors Series).

Editor's Foreword

CHAPLIN needs no introduction to film lovers. It is he who provides the definition of *auteur* against which all other contenders for that title must be measured. As Julian Smith points out, Andre Bazin articulated Chaplin's unique significance when he wrote in *What Is Cinema?*, "Chaplin is perhaps the only example to date of a creative person who has totally subordinated the cinema to what he had to say, without worrying about conforming to the specifics of its techniques." As Smith himself recalls, after Mack Sennett's *Tillie's Punctured Romance* (one durable archetype that Chaplin vastly underrated), "Chaplin would never act in front of another director's camera or appear in a role he had not written for himself." Besides writing, directing, and acting in all of his films after 1914 (even playing bit parts in those starring others), he became his own producer in control of his own studio and, after joining United Artists, had a hand in the distribution of his work. He even composed the musical scores for his films and rigidly imposed his taste on subordinate craftsmen. Through some dazzling successes and occasional failures, he proved the possibility—despite the unlikelihood—of cinema being a one-man show.

Chaplin has been much discussed in print—by himself, by flattering and hostile biographers, by film historians—especially devotees of silent comedy—by gossip columnists and bigoted opinion-makers. One may ask what remains to be said. Julian Smith's book merits attention for two principal reasons. First, like Gene Phillips's companion *Alfred Hitchcock* in this series, it corrects errors that have crept into previous accounts of the films, since it is based on a recent viewing of the entire available body of Chaplin's work. Second, it devotes proportionately more space to Chaplin's "talking pictures" than earlier studies that concentrated on Chaplin's silent shorts and gradually lengthening features culminating in *The Gold Rush*. Some admirers, Smith points out, never reconciled themselves to the abandonment of the "old Chaplin" of the slapstick comedies beginning with *The Great Dictator*, since they longed to freeze Charlie forever in the world of the silent clowns.

Since the early short films have been treated at great length and with great reverence, Smith spends less time on them than his predecessors in order to explain his high regard for the remarkable trilogy of *The Great Dictator, Monsieur Verdoux,* and *Limelight*—films that were either pointlessly controversial or ignored for wrong reasons at the time of their release.

In short, Smith provides here an account that shifts the usual critical focus on Chaplin that sees perhaps *The Gold Rush,* perhaps *Modern Times,* as his supreme achievement and instead views all the work through *Limelight* as the unique embodiment of a tragicomic vision that comes full circle by returning to death in the music hall that was the birthplace and fountainhead of Chaplin's techniques and visions.

W. F.

Preface

"TO THINK OF Charlie Chaplin is to think of the movies," says Lewis Jacobs. "Yet this unique actor, director, and producer has added little to movie technique or movie form. . . . His artistic problems have not been cinematic; they have been personal, always being solved by feeling. His importance lies not in what he has contributed to film art, but in what he has contributed to humanity."[1] This study of Chaplin will take exactly the opposite perspective by assuming that Chaplin added as much, if not more, to film form as any other major director; that his artistic problems (and their solutions) were always cinematic, never personal; and that if he contributed anything to humanity, it was through his attention to film form and technique. If I had to reduce my study of Chaplin to a single phrase, I would take it from Gerald Mast: "There has never been a better film technician than Chaplin because Chaplin's technique was perfectly suited to communicate what he wanted. And that is as good as technique can ever be."[2]

What was it, exactly, that Chaplin wanted to communicate? Nothing less, I suggest, than he communicates in the punning title of his last book about himself: *My Life in Pictures*. My central thesis, if I must admit to having one, is that Chaplin is self-referential in many of his films, particularly in his features. The self to which he refers is sometimes the private one: "I never get away from the notion that I am watching myself in the passing show," Chaplin told Mordaunt Hall in 1925; "I become, myself, a piece of film."[3] But as I will try to demonstrate throughout this study, Chaplin more frequently chose topics, settings, and characters that allowed him to explore, directly or indirectly, the nature, methods, problems and conditions of his art—and of his life as an artist who made "pictures."

Although Chaplin's active career as a major filmmaker stretched from 1914 until 1952 and although he continued making films until 1966, his earlier biographers and critics devote at least half of their attention to the period before he turned exclusively to the production of feature films with *A Woman of Paris* in 1923. One important book, *Chaplin: Genesis of a Clown*, stops in 1917. Robert Payne's study reaches its midpoint in 1916–1917, Roger Manvell's midpoint comes in 1918 with *A Dog's Life*. Chaplin's 1964 autobiography is half done by the time he gets to the editing of *The Kid* in 1920; the books by John McCabe and R. J. Minney take half their length to get to the start of Chaplin's trip abroad in 1921, while Theodore Huff's biography breaks in half with Chaplin's return from that trip. There are obvious reasons for this common emphasis on the earlier films: there are so many of them (sixty-six before *The Kid*; thirteen after); they are the films that made Chaplin and his "tramp" alter ego famous; so many of them are so good; and they provide the foundation on which any comprehensive analysis of his career must be based. This study, however, will touch as lightly (but thoroughly) as possible on the shorter films that demonstrate Chaplin's growth toward mastery of the feature-length narrative. And because I have a higher regard than most other critics for Chaplin's sound films (in which category I include *City Lights* and *Modern Times* without qualification), I will give them relatively greater attention. Thus, the midpoint of this book comes with *The Circus* (1928) on the eve of Chaplin's transition to sound.

This book will also differ from earlier studies of Chaplin in its accuracy about what actually happens in the films. Most earlier biographers were hampered by having to rely on their memories. I was fortunate to have ready access to all of the features and many of the shorter films while writing and revising this book.

Being accurate about what happens on the screen is an easy task compared with trying to be accurate about Chaplin's life and personality. The problem does not result from a lack of evidence so much as from an overabundance. No other figure in the history of film has been the subject of so much attention. And much of it was by the people who supposedly knew him best—his first two wives signed their names to sensationalized accounts; one lover devoted an entire book to him; two women he was rumored to be engaged to have provided long passages on Chaplin in their autobiographies; two of his sons published gossipy books about him; many people who worked for him in various capacities have given interviews or written articles or chapters or whole books on him—and his Japanese factotum and companion for nearly two decades, Kono, told all to a biographer after leaving Chaplin's employ.

With few exceptions, these works tell us almost nothing about the conditions under which Chaplin's films were made or how they were made—and little we can trust about the man himself. This caveat applies with equal force to the many "autobiographical" books and articles ghostwritten by Chaplin's employees. Even when we can be reasonably certain that Chaplin is the author of a publication or statement with his name on it, we must be cautious. Konrad Bercovici, recalling his friendship with Chaplin in the early 1920s, claims that "even as he talked [about the autobiography he was writing], he told four different versions of one early childhood incident. Even as he affirmed that he intended to tell the truth, the absolute truth about his life, he told two or three different truths. . . . It was all play-acting, a thousand Chaplins all revolving around a nonexistent axis."[4]

Finally, I believe I should explain that I have taken as a guiding principle Andre Bazin's warning that because Chaplin is great we must be predisposed to treat the apparent flaws in his films "as qualities . . . whose secret we have not so far been able to fathom."[5] This does not mean that I am uncritical—only that I have done everything in my power to try to understand what it is Chaplin is trying to make us see or feel.

JULIAN SMITH

University of Florida

Acknowledgments

I WISH to express my thanks to those who helped me see Chaplin's films: the staff at the Motion Picture Division of the Library of Congress, Chad Reed in the Program Office at the University of Florida's Reitz Union, and Jim Flavin in the University of Florida's Office of Instructional Resources. I am also grateful to the students in my Chaplin course, especially Jeff Dean, and to the audience at our Chaplin series for their enthusiasm—no critic of Chaplin can begin to understand what is really funny and important in Chaplin's films without seeing them in chronological order with a large and faithful audience made up of people of all ages.

Most of all, I am grateful to William C. Childers, Harry M. Geduld, and Gerald Mast for their comments and advice on all or parts of this manuscript—and to Warren French for suggesting that I do this book.

Chronology

1889	Charles Spencer Chaplin born in London, 16 April.
1901	Father dies. Chaplin begins stage career.
1907	Joins the Karno Pantomime Troupe.
1910	Arrives in United States with Karno touring company.
1913	Signs movie contract. November, last stage performance.
1914	Appears in thirty-four one- or two-reel Keystone comedies directed by himself, Mack Sennett, and others—and in *Tillie's Punctured Romance*, a feature.
1915	Makes fourteen one- and two-reel comedies for Essanay.
1916–1917	Makes twelve two-reelers for Mutual: *The Floorwalker, The Fireman, The Vagabond, One A.M., The Count, The Pawnshop, Behind the Screen, The Rink, Easy Street, The Cure, The Immigrant, The Adventurer*.
1918	In his own studio, sets out to produce eight short films for First National. *A Dog's Life* (three reels); *Shoulder Arms* (three reels). Marries Mildred Harris.
1919	*Sunnyside* (three reels). Son born but dies three days later. *A Day's Pleasure* (two reels). Helps form United Artists.
1920	Divorced by Mildred Harris on grounds of mental cruelty.
1921	*The Kid* (six reels). *The Idle Class* (two reels). Brief visit to England and Europe.
1922	*Pay Day* (two reels).
1923	Finishes First National contract with *The Pilgrim* (four reels). Turns exclusively to making features for United Artists with *A Woman of Paris*.
1924	Marries Lita Grey, who will bear him two sons.

1925	*The Gold Rush*.
1927	Divorced from Lita Grey. Has nervous breakdown.
1928	*The Circus*. Mother dies.
1931	*City Lights*. Meets Paulette Goddard.
1936	*Modern Times*. Confirms rumors of marriage to Goddard.
1940	*The Great Dictator*.
1942	Divorced by Goddard.
1943	Marries Oona O'Neill, who will bear him eight children.
1947	*Monsieur Verdoux* released during political controversy; film soon withdrawn.
1952	*Limelight*. Leaves United States.
1953	Buys new home in Switzerland. Sells Hollywood studio.
1957	*A King in New York* (made in England).
1964	*My Autobiography*.
1966	Ends his film career with *A Countess from Hong Kong* (made in England).
1972	Returns to United States to receive special Academy Award.
1975	*My Life in Pictures*. Knighted by Elizabeth II.
1977	Sir Charles Spencer Chaplin dies in his sleep on Christmas day.

1

The Long Apprenticeship

The Birth of the Art and the Artist

THE YEAR 1989 will mark the centennial of two events for which no record exists: W. K. L. Dickson's claim that he projected a film for Thomas Alva Edison, his employer—and the birth of the man who would become the greatest single practitioner of film art. Like the industry he bestrides, Chaplin's origins are lost in obscurity and confusion. Not only is there no documentary evidence of his birth, but Chaplin himself told conflicting stories. At first he claimed to have been born in France, later he reduced the claim to conception in France and birth in London, finally he dropped all foreign claims. The first chapter of *My Autobiography* opens with a surprisingly and suspiciously precise statement: "I was born on April 16, 1889, at eight o'clock at night, in East Lane, Walworth."[1]

Just as there is debate about whether motion pictures were conceived or born in France, England, or the United States, Chaplin's ethnic origins are uncertain. At various times and for various reasons, Chaplin claimed to be of Irish, Spanish, French, or Gypsy descent. Sometimes he claimed to be Jewish, at other times he insisted he was not. "As nearly as can be determined," says one recent biographer with as much certainty as anyone can muster, "Charlie Chaplin is virtually part Jewish almost most of the time."[2]

About a year after Chaplin's birth, his parents separated. His father took up with another woman and sired a son of whom we have no record other than Chaplin's memory; his mother, who had already borne one illegitimate child (Chaplin's beloved older half-brother, Sydney), had two more bastard sons by a man named Dryden. Out of all this domestic confusion, only one thing seems fairly certain: that though his parents, music hall performers Charles Chaplin and Lily Harley (née Hannah

(Top of page) Chaplin as he first appeared on the screen in Making a Living. *On the right is Henry Lehrman, who directed Chaplin's first film. (Bottom of page) Chaplin with Edna Purviance in* The Immigrant. *The woman on the far right is Henry Bergman.*

19

Hill), had five children between them, Chaplin was the only one they created together. He was, in short, an original.

Chaplin's childhood is as murky as his origins. Thomas Burke, the author of the popular *Limehouse Nights* and other tales of London lowlife, and perhaps the most astute among Chaplin's friends who tried to get him on paper, asserted that "apart from the little he himself has chosen to tell (much of it confusing), the story of his life before he discovered America is almost as misty as the story of Shakespeare's London years. . . . No man, even a man deliberately trying to hide himself, has hidden his early life as effectually as Charles."[3] Of all the stories Chaplin told about his childhood, none is more dramatic than his claim that he made his first appearance on the stage at the tender age of five after his mother suddenly lost her voice. In his first self-portrait in 1916, Chaplin tells how his father forced him onto the stage;[4] half a century later, in *My Autobiography*, the taskmaster father has disappeared and the description is gentler: "I remember standing in the wings when Mother's voice cracked and went into a whisper. The audience began to laugh and sing falsetto and to make catcalls. It was all vague and I did not quite understand what was going on. . . . And in the turmoil I remember [the stage manager] leading me by the hand and . . . leaving me on the stage alone. And before a glare of footlights and faces in smoke, I started to sing. . . . Halfway through, a shower of money poured onto the stage. Immediately I stopped and announced that I would pick up the money first and sing afterwards. This caused much laughter. . . . when mother came on the stage to carry me off, her presence evoked tremendous applause" (A, 18–19). Whether or not this story is "true" in substance or detail is unimportant. What is important is that Chaplin retold it throughout his career, perhaps because it was true, perhaps because he came to believe it was true.

Chaplin's first independently documentable stage appearance came at the age of nine in late 1898 when he began to tour the provinces with the Eight Lancashire Lads. Remaining with this clog-dancing troupe until he was eleven, Chaplin then played a street waif in a touring production of *From Rags to Riches*. In late December 1900, he first demonstrated his talent for pantomime by playing a cat in *Cinderella* at the London Hippodrome. A year later, his hard-drinking father died of cirrhosis of the liver—and his mother, who seems to have had a bout with madness when Chaplin was seven, lapsed into a more or less permanent condition of insanity and was committed to a public asylum. Though Chaplin claims to have led the life of a street waif for the next few years, there is evidence he was placed in a school.

Given the fact that Chaplin went on to create films in which the central character was usually impoverished and lived on the edge of things, it is tempting to assume that the "tramp" figure was shaped by these early experiences. But we must also be careful to remember that the young Chaplin sought for and found professional and economic success at an early age. Even granting that Chaplin's childhood contained great stretches of poverty, humiliation, and misery, there is ample evidence that it was also filled with laughter, pleasure, and good fortune.

Shortly after his fourteenth birthday, Chaplin was offered contracts for two dramatic roles that would win him his first favorable press notices. The first role was that of Sammy, a newspaper boy in a short-lived touring production of *Jim; a Romance of Cockayne*. Several weeks later, in July 1903, he began a tour as Billy, a pageboy in *Sherlock Holmes*. Having started at what was then an adult's living wage of two pounds ten shillings a week, Chaplin was so successful in the part that two years and three tours later, he was still playing Billy and was the only survivor of the original cast. Late in 1905, young Chaplin had his first major London appearance: he acted opposite the great William Gillette in a curtain-raiser at the Duke of York's Theatre, and then reenacted the role of Billy in a London revival of *Sherlock Holmes* starring Gillette.

After another provincial tour with *Sherlock Holmes* in early 1906, Chaplin was out of work for several months until he joined a touring company of *Casey's Court*, a play about Cockney slum children. That was followed by a year with the Casey Circus, a vaudeville company; "it was an awful show," Chaplin claims, "but it gave me a chance to develop as a comedian" (A, 95). After several unsuccessful efforts to find a niche for himself when he was too old to play boys on the stage and too young to play a man, Chaplin's breakthrough came shortly before his nineteenth birthday when Sydney, who had become a featured player in one of Fred Karno's comedy troupes, talked Karno into giving his younger brother a chance. Working for Karno meant an opportunity to learn and refine a variety of burlesque, slapstick, and pantomime techniques that would later prove useful in Hollywood. It also meant learning respect for the kind of tireless rehearsal and careful preparation that was almost unheard of in the early days of moviemaking. Equally important, Karno insisted on the mingling of comedy and pathos that would mark Chaplin's greatest films. Stan Laurel, who worked in the same Karno company as Chaplin, remembers their mentor exhorting his players to "Keep it wistful, gentlemen, keep it *wistful*. . . . we want sympathy with the laughter.'[5]

In the summer of 1908, Chaplin reached his first international audience in Paris when he appeared at the Folies Bergeres in a Karno sketch. Back in England, he perfected his craft in leading and supporting roles in a great variety of pantomime sketches. Finally, in late 1910 the twenty-one-year-old Chaplin arrived in the United States for the first of two American tours. Shortly after his arrival, Chaplin and Alf Reeves, the manager of the touring company, began to frequent movies in New York and to talk about forming a partnership to make film versions of Karno sketches—but the prudent, skeptical Reeves talked him out of such a scheme. Seven or eight years later, Alf Reeves would become general manager of Chaplin's studio.

Chaplin's "discovery" by the infant film industry is the stuff of legend. The most popular version, told in various forms by Chaplin and Mack Sennett, is that Sennett spotted him as a drunken dandy in a sketch entitled *A Night in an English Music Hall*—and that Sennett made the discovery either while he was still an actor working for D. W. Griffith at the Biograph Studios in New York or just after he took charge of the new Keystone Studio in suburban Los Angeles.

However it happened, we know that Chaplin ended nearly six years of association with Karno after a final performance in Kansas City on 29 November 1913 and signed a contract with Keystone for a starting salary of $125 a week, about five times the top salary a Ford Motor Company employee would have earned on a different assembly line. Chaplin claims he took the new job with cold-blooded calculation: "Had I seen a Keystone Comedy? asked [one of Keystone's owners]. Of course, I had seen several, but I did not tell him that I thought they were a crude mélange of rough-and-tumble. . . . I was not terribly enthusiastic about the Keystone type of comedy, but I realized their publicity value. A year at that racket and I could return to vaudeville an international star" (*A*, 138). It would be nearly forty years before he abandoned California—and more than half a century before he made his last film.

Without knowing it, Chaplin was entering the movie "racket" at one of its most chaotic and creative periods. The star system was still in its infancy, a bare three years old, and the industry was on the verge of shifting from the short film to the longer format that we now call the "feature." Sennett's old mentor, D. W. Griffith, who began his film career as an actor the same year Chaplin joined the Karno Company, had just rebelled against his superiors at Biograph by producing the "epic" *Judith of Bethulia* instead of churning out his quota of one-reelers. As if that was not bold enough, Griffith had also demanded a larger salary, a share of the profits, and more control over his output. Biograph fired Griffith, but even as Chaplin was learning the ropes at Keystone, Griffith was making *The Birth of a Nation* on the other side of town, thereby proving that a genuine artist could not and should not be controlled by the businessmen back in New York. Griffith would win his battle—and Chaplin would be one of the first beneficiaries of the victory.

The Year with Keystone

"Of all the great figures, and there are many, that the cinema has produced, Charles Chaplin is the most certain of immortality," says J. H. Plumb. "He had the luck, as all great artists must have, to be in the heroic age of a new art."[6] He also, as Horatio Alger would put it, had the pluck. It is noteworthy that in *Making a Living*, his first film, Chaplin plays a confidence man, a swindler—and that the director of the film, Henry "Pathé" Lehrman, was something of a con-man himself, having gotten his nickname as a result of talking his way into his first film job by claiming to be the American representative of Pathé Frères, the famous French film company. When Lehrman set out to direct Chaplin, he probably thought that he was in control of the film, just as he probably thought that the handsome young reporter he plays was the central character. But Chaplin, who had been cast as the troublemaker who keeps the plot moving, stole the picture from his director—just as the character he played stole the reporter's camera containing a "scoop" photograph of an accident.

As the film opens, a stock comic villain stands waiting for opportunity to present itself. Disguised in a top hat, sinisterly drooping mustache, cravat, long frock coat, pipestem trousers, and tight little shoes with raised heels, he springs into action when Lehrman walks into frame and stops because he has stepped in something disgusting. Most viewers today will not recognize the mugging, leering, constantly talking figure as Chaplin, but at the end of the first scene, when the con man turns his back to the camera and prances off, the delicate, precise Chaplin walk is unmistakeable, the famous kinetic icon fully formed against the whiteness of the sidewalk.

Most of what follows is frantic, pointless knockabout leading to a chase down the middle of a crowded street. But anyone who can screen in chronological order the Biograph comedies directed by Griffith and his protégé Sennett, and then the early Keystones directed by Sennett and his protégés, will recognize that something entirely new, unexpected, and transcendent is happening in Chaplin's debut. We see it in the way Chaplin kisses an old editor on his bald head and then not only pounds on the old man's knee for emphasis but yanks the knee back when the editor pulls it away in annoyance, in the way he uses his supple cane to hold off the angry Lehrman, in the way he jumps on the backs and shoulders of a crowd to see what it is looking at—and in the process forces us to look at him. Taken together, these grace notes establish that Chaplin, the new player, and not Lehrman, the experienced director, is in control of the film, of the audience, and of himself.

In *My Autobiography*, Chaplin claims that the few bits of funny business he invented for their second film together were mutilated by Lehrman in the cutting room. But a close look at that film reveals that Lehrman had enough appreciation for what Chaplin was capable of doing to provide him with a clever narrative framework in which he could explore his proper relationship to the camera and his audience. Let us try to imagine seeing the film when it first came out in early 1914. The long, geographically specific title—Kid Auto Races at Venice— suggests that we are about to see a documentary. The first shot begins with Chaplin in frame at the edge of a crowd. Because he was unknown at this point, he would seem to us, the original audience, to be nothing more than a rather oddly dressed idler—a recipient, perhaps, of random scraps of sartorial charity. When an apparently real cop tells him to stand somewhere else, this figure in the tight jacket and baggy trousers tips his hat, thus calling attention to how small it is and how lightly it sits upon his head. Moving to the middle of the race track, he hears someone yell at him, turns around, acknowledges the camera, struts out of frame, then back. Again told to move on, he points inquiringly in one direction, then goes in the other.

The second shot is a kind of visual "chaser": because Chaplin is not in frame and the camera shows racing cars from the point of view of the grandstand, we could assume that the strange-looking figure is just a bystander who has nothing to do with the purpose of the "documentary." We are, of course, simply being set up by Lehrman (or Chaplin) for the third shot: after panning past several spectators who are hiding their faces from the camera while many others stare directly at it (thus reinforcing the notion we are watching a documentary), the camera discovers Chaplin sitting with the crowd. Again acknowledging the camera, he gets up in order to stay in front of it until an angry Henry Lehrman rushes into frame and pushes him out of view. Popping back into frame, Chaplin begins to pose. Again, Lehrman pushes him out of frame; again Chaplin returns. And now, perhaps for the first if not the only time in the history of the film, we see a real audience's actual discovery of a major new artist: many in the crowd that had gathered to watch the race have forgotten the cars speeding by and are watching Chaplin. It is the children who first notice him and smile, then the adults.

Once Lehrman establishes that Chaplin, not the race, is his subject, he lets the audience in on the joke. Thus, the fourth shot is from the point of view of a camera behind the camera being directed by Lehrman (who must have had something of a sense of humor to mock himself in this way). And so it goes for shot after shot as Lehrman works variations on the joke of Chaplin hogging the camera in spite of being cajoled, threatened, shoved, chased, knocked down, chased some more. But he keeps coming back for more—and would for another fifty-two years in front of his own cameras.

By looking into the camera, by ignoring the anger of the make-believe and actual director who was trying to control him, Chaplin and his nameless character (assuming the two are somehow different in this case) rise above the artificiality of the movie itself, above the mechanical technique of filmmaking. In *Kid Auto Races at Venice*, Chaplin establishes a direct personal relationship with the audience, a relationship that shows that he does not belong in the world of Keystone and is only an outsider passing through on his way to greatness. More than anything else, he demonstrates here that he intends to do things his own way.

Sennett had hired Chaplin to replace Ford Sterling, a large, blustering actor who played cops, swindlers, philandering husbands, and other stock types. But no one at Keystone quite knew what to do with Chaplin, who was much smaller and younger than Sterling. As we have seen, Chaplin's first screen appearance was as a stock type: an opportunist conventionally motivated by the desire for money and female company. By the time he appeared on the screen again, five days later in *Kid Auto Races*, Chaplin had made a quantum leap from stock Keystone character to a screen original: an inexplicable, motiveless, self-centered, bizarre, lonely, and compelling presence with more than a touch of madness. To a large extent, this persona was a product of the costume Chaplin invented for a film that went into production before *Kid Auto Races* but was released later. In *My Autobiography*, Chaplin describes how, after Sennett ordered him to put on a comedy makeup for a bit part in *Mabel's Strange Predicament*, "I had no idea what make-up to put on. . . . However, on the way to the wardrobe I thought I would dress in baggy pants, big shoes, a cane and a derby hat. I wanted everything a contradiction: the pants baggy, the coat tight, the hat small and the shoes large. I was undecided whether to look old or young, but remembering Sennett had expected me to be a much older man, I added a small mustache, which, I reasoned, would add age without hiding my expression" (*A*, 144).

Thus was born the basic "costume" and the little mustache Chaplin would use for the next twenty-six years. Between the time he invented this costume in early 1914 and the time he last wore it as the barber in *The Great Dictator*, the world would enter two great wars. When he put the costume on, D. W. Griffith was making *The Birth of a Nation;* when he put it aside, Orson Welles was about to make *Citizen Kane*.

Having invented the costume, Chaplin tells us, "I had no idea of the character. But the moment I was dressed, the clothes and the make-up made me feel the person he was. I began to know him, and by the time I walked onto the stage he was fully born" (*A*, 144). Though it is satisfying to believe that the costume had somehow created the archetypal Chaplin persona of the shabby, impoverished outsider, the truth is that for the next three years and sixty films, Chaplin would usually play someone who had a home or a job—and sometimes a wife and family.

The "basic" costume did, however, supply an instant trademark. Although Chaplin would occasionally abandon it during the year he spent with Keystone (he would also play a frumpy woman, a man masquerading as a woman, a rich swell, a conventional city slicker, and a bear-skinned caveman with an anachronistic cane and derby), the general rule seems to have been quickly established: he would wear some version of the costume established for his second film unless there was a compelling reason to wear something else because of the setting, story, or characterization. And even when he became, for example, a cop, a parson, or a soldier, the fit and cut of the new costume would remind us of the famous old one.

In April 1914, after playing parts in nearly a dozen films, Chaplin was allowed to write and co-direct *Caught in a Cabaret*. From that point on, he directed or co-directed all but a handful of his remaining films with Keystone and was indisputably the central attraction in all but two. The two exceptions are worth attention because they remind us that Chaplin was working in a repertory company. In *The Knockout*, a Fatty Arbuckle vehicle, Chaplin does not appear until the last third of the film. But what an entrance he makes as the referee: he occupies the center of the stage where the ring is located, spreads his arms in that little "da-DUM!" gesture of victory we see in later films like *The Pawnshop*, and promptly falls through the ropes into the ring. Once the boxing match starts, Chaplin gets knocked down by wild punches, trips Fatty and counts him out, falls to his knees and begs for mercy. When Chaplin disappears from the action, the film turns into a routine Keystone Kops chase. His cameo appearance here is a metaphor for his year at Keystone: he came late, brought some order and style to the proceedings, and left before the place fell apart. The other exception is *Tillie's Punctured Romance*. Conceived as a starring role for the massive Marie Dressler, Keystone's newest acquisition, this six-reeler was probably the first feature-length comedy and is still worth viewing in spite of Chaplin's negative assessment: "It was pleasant working with Marie, but I did not think the picture had much merit" (A, 158). What he probably means is that there is not enough of him in the farce and that he was required to subordinate his character to the overwhelming presence of Dressler, who is largely responsible for the film's continued popularity. After *Tillie's Punctured Romance*, Chaplin would never act in front of another director's camera or appear in a role he had not written for himself, except in cameo roles of his own choosing.

The Year at Essanay

Though Chaplin could have gone on writing and directing his own comedies at Keystone, he would have been under the heavy hand of Mack Sennett, wasting energy better spent on his films in fighting for control over his work. He precipitated the break with Keystone by demanding a new salary of $1,000 a week, which was more than Sennett made—and less than others were willing to pay: the Essanay Company offered him $1,250 a week and a bonus of $10,000. After a trip to the dreary northern California "studio" where G. M. Anderson, the co-owner and "A" of Essanay, made his "Bronco Billy" Westerns, Chaplin went to Chicago where George K. Spoor (the "S") ran the head office. There he made *His New Job*, a self-referential quickie about getting a job at the "Lockstone" studio (the opposite, obviously, of "Keystone"). Building his scriptless film around the activities of a studio allowed Chaplin to discover what and who it was he had to work with. His chief discovery was Roland H. ("Rollie") Totheroh, the cameraman who would work on all of his films for the next thirty-two years.

After finishing his first film at the Chicago studios, Chaplin decided that Bronco Billy Anderson's dusty, makeshift studio in the countryside near San Francisco was preferable to working in Chicago, so he left for California, bringing with him Totheroh and some of the actors he had used in *His New Job*, most notably Ben Turpin and Leo White. He did not bother to take along the young actress he had briefly considered as a possible leading lady, Gloria Swanson. Back in California, he searched for a leading lady and finally settled on Edna Purviance, a twenty-one year old who had never appeared in a film. A perfect visual and emotional foil to Chaplin, placid where he is manic, fully formed against his slightness, radiantly blond to his darkness, eternally female, Miss Purviance (the name rhymes with "reliance") soon became famous around the world as "Edna," the name by which she was referred to in the intertitle cards. She would play the romantic feminine lead opposite Chaplin in all of his films for the next eight years, but would be replaced when her youthful lushness turned matronly on the eve of her thirtieth year.

Through the winter and into the early spring of 1915, Chaplin made five comedies at the northern California studio. The first four were, like *His New Job*, variations on the kind of work he had done for Sennett and repeat specific gags and situations from the Keystone comedies. *A Jitney Elopement*, the fourth in the series, is the most interesting today because it shows the conventionally antic direction Chaplin might have taken had he not stumbled down the dusty road that led him eventually to *A Dog's Life* and *The Kid*. After a vulgar dinner scene in which

Chaplin makes jokes about the windy effects of eating beans, "the
musical fruit," the action moves to a park where bricks get thrown, then
into a car chase that looks more dangerous than funny; finally, Chaplin's
version of the Keystone Kops gets into the act and authority ends up
taking a dunk in the ocean.

There is one small detail in *A Jitney Elopement* that suggests Chaplin
was in the process of discovering something new about himself and his
persona: after we meet Edna and learn that she is about to be forced to
marry someone she does not love, an iris opens'to introduce the Chaplin
character standing under her window, sniffing a flower. For just a few
seconds, we get the most fleeting impression of wistful pathos, but it is
soon forgotten. Chaplin would expand on that flash of pathos in his very
next film by creating the wistful, ultimately selfless, long-suffering
figure who is most often (and often mistakenly) referred to as the
"Tramp"—and who will be called "Charlie" in this study.

In *My Autobiography*, Chaplin claims to have defined the "Tramp"
character for Sennett within minutes of putting on the famous "costume"
for the first time: "You know this fellow is many sided, a tramp, a
gentleman, a poet, a dreamer, a lonely fellow, always hopeful of romance
and adventure" (A, 144). If he did indeed tell Sennett all these things in
early 1914, it was not until the spring of 1915 that he finally allowed this
figure to surface in *The Tramp*, a film that set new standards for characterization, mood, and construction. For one thing, it opens and closes on
a dusty road, providing Chaplin with his first classically "Chaplinesque"
ending: the Tramp walking away alone into the distance, into legend.

That ending is foreshadowed at the very start when, after two speeding cars knock the Tramp down with the wind of their passage, he gets
up, dusts himself off with a wiskbroom, and continues on his way. At the
end, "knocked down" by the careless momentum of Edna's love for
another man, he returns to the same dusty road and looks backward
toward the farm house where he left the girl he had started to love.
Favoring the leg wounded when he saved Edna and her father's farm
from a gang of hobos, he limps away from us, taking exactly ten paces
before he stops and does a little jig in place to crank up the motor of his
jauntiness. When he steps off again, the spring is back in his walk, his
confidence intact—and a great career ahead of him, for Charlie has been
born.

In most of his films before *The Tramp*, Chaplin played someone who
had a job, a home, sometimes even a wife. If he did not have a job, it was
often because he seemed to prefer the life of the swindler, con man, or
rogue. Here, for the first time, he plays someone who is specifically and
unambiguously defined as homeless on the road of life. Looking back

over his career, we can now understand that the characterization in this film is seminal because it provides a point of departure for the wistful, gentle figures in *The Kid, The Gold Rush, The Circus, City Lights, Modern Times, The Great Dictator,* and *Limelight*. And yet, as we turn to his next films, we will see that he may not have been fully aware of exactly what he had accomplished in *The Tramp*. It would take more than a year and another ten films before he would give us a similar homeless figure in *The Vagabond*.

After finishing *The Tramp*, Chaplin moved his base of operations to Los Angeles to free himself from conflicts with Bronco Billy Anderson over space and authority. Bringing with him many of the people who had worked on his first five Essanay films, he began to pick up other players. Over the next year or two, his basic repertory company would stabilize around a few favorite cast and crew who would, like the Globe company around Shakespeare, inspire and compel him to repeat with infinite variety certain character types, conflicts, and situations.

Having caught the first glimmerings of "Charlie" in *The Tramp*, he spent the rest of the year refining and defining this new persona in relation to the world around him, the respectable world that would always exclude him. After grinding out *By the Sea*, a one-reel farce that seems another throwback to Keystone (that it is a one-reeler is important: he would never again make anything shorter than two reels), Chaplin dramatically slowed his rate of production from several films a month to about one a month for the remainder of the year. One sign of this slower rate of production is the extreme care he gives in his next three films—*Work, A Woman,* and *The Bank*—to the problem of introducing Charlie in a way that establishes in visual terms who and what he is.

At the start of *Work*, Charlie is silhouetted against the sky as he pulls a heavily loaded wagon up a steep slope. The starkness and simplicity of the image reduces Charlie to a cartoon Sisyphus, a horseless Don Quixote tilting against gravity. This striking graphic design is not, however, functional, for although the little-man-against-the-sky image is heavily loaded with symbolic import, the story that follows soon turns into a knockabout farce that is probably based on *Repairs*, a Karno sketch.

In *A Woman*, Chaplin found a perfect way to foreshadow the surprising shape of things to come by having Charlie make an almost mythic entrance out of the heart of lightness. The setting is a park and the camera is waiting expectantly as Charlie's approaching figure forms itself out of the glare, much like the figures that emerge from the light flooding out of the spaceship in *Close Encounters of the Third Kind*. Here, the sticklike, unfocused figure of Charlie takes on more and more shape as he gets closer, and, passing through the light-refracting spray of a lawn sprinkler, fills the frame from top to bottom.

Charlie's shifty, out-of-focus entrance prepares us for the transitory, intangible nature of the figure he plays. In short, it warns us that he can become anything he wants, or anything we or the characters around him think he is. In this case, he becomes the "woman" of the title. Let us look at the stages of this remarkable transformation. First a blindfolded man thinks Charlie is the pretty girl who put him in the dark; then Charlie sits on a feathered hat and struts around like a chicken when the hat pin jabs him. Having been mistaken for a woman and having briefly worn a woman's hat at the wrong end of his anatomy, Charlie next puts on a dress to hide himself from his enemies. Finally, he shaves off his mustache and puts on makeup to complete the transformation.

With his large, dramatic eyes and painted lips, Chaplin is absolutely convincing as a woman, and therein lies the problem he was facing in those days: what kind of character should he be when he could be anyone or anything? At the start of *The Bank,* we find the answer to that question locked away like a great treasure. Entering the bank with a proprietary air of great confidence and purpose, Charlie opens the vault and takes out the objective correlatives of his identity: a mop and bucket. Having established the conceptual basis for his humor in the disparity between the confident image Charlie projects and the reality of his janitorial position, Chaplin then proceeds to demonstrate that there was indeed a treasure in the vault: the thematic and comic possibilities of a mere mop in the hands of an artist who could turn a small investment in celluloid into piles of silver and gold. At the end, rejected by Edna, Charlie goes to sleep and dreams that he saves her from bank robbers and locks them in the vault he opened at the start. Edna melts into his arms and he awakens to find he is stroking and kissing the mop. At the start, his air of importance is only an illusion; at the end, romance is only a dream. At each point, it is the lowly mop that brings him (and us) back to reality.

Toward the end of his contract with Essanay, Chaplin began to make a feature about which little is known except that it was to be called "Life" and would, in the guess-work reconstruction of John McCabe, "show the tragicomic world of flophouses, grimy alleys, and living 'on the beg.'"[7] But pressure from the Essanay front office for a steady supply of two-reelers kept him busy. In the three films he made after *The Bank,* we see how Chaplin handled the pressure: he borrows cross-cutting techniques from *The Birth of a Nation* for *Shanghaied,* steals directly from Karno's *A Night in an English Music Hall* for *A Night in the Show,* and cashes in on the success of Cecil B. DeMille's *Carmen* by making a burlesque.

Eventually, he abandoned the projected feature; all that remains of "Life" is to be found in *Triple Trouble*, the pastiche of Chaplin footage Essanay compiled and released two years after Chaplin moved on to Mutual.

Though the year with Essanay was one of the most eventful and crucial in his life, in *My Autobiography* Chaplin mentions only three of his fourteen Essanay comedies (as opposed to all twelve of his Mutuals), and none with any pride or enthusiasm. Looking back over some of the films Chaplin made after he moved back to Los Angeles, we can see clues that would delight a Marxist critic searching for images of exploitation: in *Work*, Charlie is an undersized beast of burden; the drab janitor surrounded by the wealth and glamour of the bank fights back in the only way he can, with incompetence, laziness, and a final pathetic flight into the fantasy that he has some value in the marketplace; in *Shanghaied*, a corrupt businessman wants to blow up his ship to collect the insurance. Contemplating the last of the Essanay films, the Marxist critic would die and go to heaven, for in *Police* Chaplin plays a convict released from the security of the prison where he had been fed, sheltered, and protected into a world of hunger, exploitation, and danger. But he is, of course, free—and so was Chaplin.

The Mutual Period

When Chaplin finished his contract with Essanay at the end of 1915, he sent his brother Sydney to New York, the financial center of the film industry, to negotiate the best possible terms for a new contract. Sydney struck an astounding bargain with the Mutual Film Corporation, the distributing company for which D. W. Griffith had made *The Birth of a Nation*. Mutual would pay Chaplin $10,000 a week plus a bonus of $150,000. The salary was unprecedented in the world of entertainment and there was some resentment because this recent immigrant in his mid-twenties would be earning almost as much in a single year as the entire United States Senate.

With the signing of the contract to deliver twelve two-reel comedies, Chaplin entered what he calls "the happiest period of my career. I was light and unencumbered, twenty-seven years old, with fabulous prospects and a friendly, glamorous world before me" (A, 188). Master of the Lone Star Studio (he was the Lone Star, a Texas unto himself), secure in the affection of Edna Purviance, he was world famous—an important British magazine would, that year, proclaim that "the lineaments of Mr. Chaplin are known to the uttermost ends of the earth and his face may be described as one upon which the sun never sets."[8]

But even before this *annus mirabilis* began, Chaplin was to learn the burdens of sudden fame, of involuntary servitude to the public. Mobbed in Amarillo, Kansas City, and Chicago on a transcontinental journey to join Sydney in New York, he had to sneak off the train before it pulled into Grand Central Station. Fifty years later, the unreality of it all was still overwhelming: "I had always thought I would like the public's attention, and here it was—paradoxically isolating me with a depressing sense of loneliness" (A, 177); "That evening I stood with the crowd in Times Square as the news flashed on the electric sign that ran around the Times Building. It read: 'Chaplin signs with Mutual at $670,000 a year.' I stood and read it objectively as though it were about someone else" (A, 179).

Chaplin's career was on a runaway escalator and in the first Mutual comedy, *The Floorwalker*, we find Charlie forced to consider riding a tricky escalator in order to return a fortune stolen by a floorwalker who looks so much like him that he thinks he is looking into a mirror. The back and forth nature of the plot, the reversals of identity, the way Charlie shifts from pesky customer to officious functionary, are all beautifully summarized in the central escalator prop that Chaplin built before he even had a story.

The Floorwalker, which went into production about three months after Chaplin finished his last film for Essanay, established the new standards under which Chaplin would labor: there was more time to make each movie and thus more time to develop gags and themes within each story; because he had full artistic control and bigger budgets, the sets were more elaborate, the lighting and camerawork more precise, the supporting casts larger and more talented. Largest and most talented of Chaplin's new players was Eric Campbell, a six-foot-four, three hundred pound giant whose ability to project vast menace on the screen was an ideal visual, psychological, and emotional counterpoint to the delicate, vulnerable image projected by Chaplin. On screen, Campbell played a series of nasty heavies who wanted to savage Charlie, ravage Edna, or both; off screen, the shy, gentle Campbell, who was also a Karno veteran, seems to have been among Chaplin's closest associates, together with two other assistants and players who joined Chaplin that year: Henry Bergman and Albert Austin.

Writing about *A Dog's Life*, the first film he made after finishing his Mutual contract, Chaplin would claim "I was beginning to think of comedy in a structural sense, and to become conscious of its architectural form. Each sequence implied the next sequence, all of them relating to the whole" (A, 209). In *The Floorwalker*, we see that he was already thinking about the structure of his comedies. But when we turn to the next Mutual, *The Fireman*, we find little attention to structure and form. To be sure, the gags are appropriate to the setting (as when Charlie fills coffee cups from the boiler of the steam engine that drives the pump mechanism), but the total effect is reminiscent of Keystone—and his reliance on stop motion, undercranking, and other camera tricks for comic effect is a clue that he was not devoting enough attention to solving the problem of telling a human story. Our eyes may be delighted by the use of reverse motion to show the effortless climbing of a pole by Eric Campbell, who could never have hoisted that great bulk up a slippery pole, but the gag is still mechanical and empty of human or narrative meaning.

As soon, however, as we turn to the next film, all is forgiven, for in *The Vagabond* we see the shape of things to come. The first two scenes, through their extreme contrasts and apparent lack of connection, suggest that Chaplin was on his way to the kind of complexity we find in his features. First we see Charlie, the vagabond fiddler whose efforts to play for a living are drowned out by the noise of an entire brass band. When he tries to collect a few coins from the patrons in a tavern, the bandsmen drive him away. Without explanation, Chaplin suddenly cuts to a rich woman grieving for the daughter stolen by Gypsies many years before. What has the downcast woman to do with the outcast musician? The major studies and synopses make no reference to the apparent non-sequitur of the grieving mother; instead, they tend to reconstruct the narrative by "cutting" from the first scene, in which the fiddler is driven away, to the third scene, in which he encounters Edna, the Gypsy drudge. In doing so, they miss the point: the vagabond fiddler is a victim who combines the sorrows of both the mother and the daughter. Like the mother, he will lose the girl; like the girl, he has been driven or torn from his proper surroundings.

The third scene opens with Edna being threatened with a bullwhip by her Gypsy taskmaster (Eric Campbell) as Charlie approaches. Apparently ignoring Edna, who is weeping into her washtub, her very tears adding to the medium of her drudgery, he begins to play his violin, which causes Edna to pause in her work and look wistful, thus creating in her and revealing to us the sensitive, "artistic" nature that will eventually result in her "discovery" by a handsome young painter. But as Charlie plays on, she begins to scrub her laundry to his mad rhythm and spills her washtub.

Calling the tunes now, Charlie rescues Edna from the Gypsy band and turns her into a composition he thinks is all his own. But by washing her face and arranging her hair, he is creating an inspiration for the spiritually hungry artist played by Chaplin's constant alter ego, Lloyd Bacon. (Bacon, who went on to become a competent director, frequently "mirrored" Charlie: he played Charlie's look-alike in *The Floorwalker*, the handsome suitor who gets Edna in *The Tramp*, and the dope addict who tries to rape her in *Easy Street*.) While Edna is nourishing the artist's spirit with her beauty, Charlie is back at the caravan, preparing a lunch that is a work of art in itself. Having transformed the drudge, he now transforms her washtub and a bit of laundry (a checkered shirt) into a table set for two—to which she invites the hungry artist.

Chaplin plays this mock idyll for laughs, but the tears are never far away—no further than vagabond Charlie's realization that the little world he has created will be plucked from him just as surely as he was overpowered by the brass band at the start. Near the end of Chaplin's first essay into pathos, the Tramp had looked back and forth between the faces of Edna and her lover. Now Chaplin escalates the effect in a shot that is equaled only by the end of *City Lights*: while Edna looks after the departing artist, her face suffused with joy, Charlie looks at her, looks at the artist, looks back at her, and then stares into the middle distance. The shot lasts barely half a minute, but it seems an eternity.

Whereas in *The Tramp* the arrival of the handsome suitor was merely a fortuitous plot point, in this film the artist does not arrive until Charlie has completed the first stage of the transformation of the drudge. Here, Edna the character is to Charlie what Edna the actress was to Chaplin: a formless lump of human clay, a blank canvas, the raw material of his art. In *The Tramp*, the hobos had merely wanted to steal her money; here, the Gypsy chief has stolen her identity, transforming the rich girl into a dirty, vermin-infested human washing machine. Now, the vagabond fiddler and the wandering painter restore her identity. When Edna looks after the painter, turning away from the fiddler, she is literally between two artists, a work in progress. The next step is that the painter completes the release of the inner beauty the fiddler found under the dirt. Chaplin opens a new scene on a close-up of the painting of Edna, then pulls back to reveal that art critics are admiring it, then even further back to reveal the entire gallery of paintings as the artist is congratulated for winning first prize. The strands of the plot come together when the grieving mother introduced in the second scene recognizes the birthmark on the bare shoulder of the "living shamrock" in the painting. With the shamelessly Victorian conceit that the artist's idealized vision retains enough of the truth for a mother, Chaplin rushes to a mechanical conclusion: Edna is carried away from Charlie in her mother's limousine. The saddened Charlie is left alone—but a moment later, after Edna becomes hysterical at the idea of leaving Charlie behind, the limousine returns and Charlie is yanked inside without ceremony.

A month after Charlie disappeared into the limousine at the end of *The Vagabond*, Chaplin gets out of a taxi to do a solo performance as a rich drunk in *One A.M.* Built around the drunk's efforts to get into his house, upstairs, and into bed, this film is a showcase for Chaplin's agility, a celebration of the intoxication of pure motion uncomplicated by the demands of romance, pathos, or plot. Like *One A.M.*, the next four films released in 1916 lack the emotional tension that drives *The Vagabond*, but they are full of individual moments that delight and astound. In *Behind the Screen*, for instance, studio prop-man Charlie notices a male statue staring at an undraped female statue—so he puts the male statue behind a screen, thus punning on the title. Then, mocking his own mock prudishness, he drops a fringed lampshade around the hips of a small nude statue and sets the lampshade in motion like the grass skirt of a hula dancer. Not content to let the gag stop there, he picks up the statue and peeks under the very same "skirt."

Everything is unstable in these five movies, as vertiginous and shifty as the rugs, stairs, revolving table, and Murphy bed in *One A.M.* In *The Count*, Charlie's boss sets out to be a fake count, but is forced to let Charlie play the part. In *The Pawnshop*, a piece of string on the floor becomes as perilous as a high wire, the teetering ladder gag still has the power to make an audience uneasy, and an alarm clock provides the opportunity for a much-admired visual essay on the power of free association. In *Behind the Screen*, Edna's disguise as a boy leads to suspicions that Charlie is a homosexual, and just about everyone in the cast falls through a particularly tricky trap door. The sequence of deception climaxes in *The Rink*, where the schemes of various philandering spouses and Charlie literally collide at the skating rink of the title—a rink where Charlie demonstrates his ability to keep moving in a slippery world where others fall prey to instability.

Five months after *The Vagabond*, and after making five films in which unreal characters occupy a fantasy world where anything is possible for the sake of a gag, Chaplin returned to the "real" world in *Easy Street*. Once again, Charlie is a derelict—but more pathetic than we have ever seen him before. Huddled in a corner under the stairs leading to the "Hope Mission," he is aroused from his sleep or despair by Edna's singing. Slowly, hesitantly entering the mission, he is immediately stuck in a series of comically embarrassing situations that contrast the sentimentality of his attraction to Edna. Shortly after a huge close-up of the wistful, love-struck Charlie responding to a smile from Edna, we see him sitting between the preacher and Edna, who is holding his left hand in her lap while he clutches his bowler to his lap with his other hand. When he stands up, he still keeps the bowler clasped to his groin to hide the shameful secret that he exposes when he pulls the collection box out of his trousers. (This priapic joke prefigures the fecundity gag involving the scrawny little man who has so many children that Charlie pins a

badge on him for achievement—and is echoed in the final action in
which Charlie saves Edna from being raped by a dope addict.) Leaving
the mission with his eyes turned heavenward, Charlie stumbles on the
steps and nearly falls on his face. These two very realistic little jokes set
the tone for the rest of *Easy Street*.

Under the divine inspiration of Edna, Charlie now undergoes the
most startling and radical conversion in any of Chaplin's films. He
becomes a policeman and imposes his own brand of order on the chaos of
Easy Street. Or, to be more precise, he supplants the brutal control of
the bully played by Eric Campbell with his own gentle control.
Noteworthy is the fact that as soon as Charlie defeats the bully at the
revolutionary intersection of Easy Street and Marie Antoinette Alley, he
frightens the denizens in the same way that the bully did—and then
proceeds to steal food for the bully's wife. The mechanism of Charlie's
final victory is a perfect summary of this film's marvellously disordered
order: cast down into a basement by a mob, Charlie sits on the drug-
addict's hypodermic syringe, then flies into a drug-induced frenzy that
restores order and brings about the happy ending in which the nightmare of bullies and drug addicts has been replaced by what Karl Marx
might have called the opium dream of the masses: the bully and all the
rest join Charlie and Edna at the new mission that has opened at the end
of Easy Street.

Whereas the first nine Mutual films were released on a regular basis,
exactly one a month from May 1916 until January 1917, there was a
three-month hiatus between *Easy Street* and the next film. In several
autobiographical works, Chaplin drops gratuitous hints about "time off
for illness" during the Mutual period.[9] Still talking about the same
period, he drops other hints: "writing, acting and directing fifty-two
weeks in the year was strenuous, requiring an exorbitant expenditure of
nervous energy. At the completion of a picture I would be left depressed
and exhausted, so that I would have to rest in bed for a day" (A, 207);
"How does one get ideas? By sheer perseverance to the point of madness" (A, 211). Whatever happened during those three lost months—
physical or emotional exhaustion or a simple determination to devote
more time to each project—the next film is set in a luxurious sanitarium
where Chaplin plays a rich, well-dressed drunk whose only link to
Charlie is the mustache.

A film of great formal unity, *The Cure* begins with an iris opening to
reveal the circular basin of the spring from which the sanitarium's guests
dip the curative waters. After the chaos caused by the dumping of our
hero's liquor supply into the basin, the film ends with the now-reformed
(or at least sober) drunk and Edna arm in arm in front of the basin as a

second iris closes in on the scene. But for all the elegance of the form, there is little life in *The Cure*—and no Charlie.

After *The Cure*, and until the end of his American career in 1952, Chaplin would never again play a member of the idle rich or ruling class unless (as in *The Idle Class* and *The Great Dictator*) he also played Charlie or a variant of that basic role. Even the elegant hero of *Monsieur Verdoux* is Charlie translated into French, a humble man driven to insane extremes. As though signaling his return to the derelict or vagrant character he had begun to experiment with in *The Tramp*, he now essayed that most archetypically homeless, outcast, and yet hopeful of characters, an immigrant on the way to America.

Like *The Vagabond* and *Easy Street*, *The Immigrant* offered Chaplin an ideal opportunity for an extended narrative. The episodic adventures of an itinerant musician in the country, a rooky cop in a slum, or an immigrant at sea and ashore could have been easily expanded to feature length, but because his contract called for two-reelers, Chaplin had to content himself with reducing the story of the immigrant to two basic sets and situations: meeting the girl (Edna Purviance) on the ship and getting involved with her; meeting her again in a restaurant in his new country.

The tilting boat set, like the teetering cabin in *The Gold Rush*, also offered an ideal opportunity for physical humor. With more experience and more time to develop his ideas, Chaplin would turn the teetering cabin into a practical representation of the basic instability of the world and of social relationships within that world—and into one of the best cliffhangers ever filmed. Here, under much tighter constraints, Chaplin still manages to pluck his story, physical and visual gags, and thematic values out of the single most obvious condition of being at sea: the movement of the ship. After establishing the ship on the stormy sea, Chaplin shows us the huddled masses of miserable passengers on the open deck, then the girl and her dying mother, and finally the familiar figure in the baggy pants. His back to us, Charlie (or one of his European cousins) is hanging over the rail of the ship, heaving and jerking in what looks like violent *mal de mer*. But when he straightens up and turns around, smiling toward us as though posing for the camera that has been capturing these "documentary" images, we see that he has caught a fish (at the very end, he makes an even bigger catch in the middle of another storm: he picks the girl up and carries her across the threshold of the marriage license bureau). After developing a number of gags about the "rolling" motion of the ship (comic seasickness, the difficulty of eating when plates slide back and forth), Chaplin cuts to a dice game after an intertitle that announces "more rolling." More than a sight gag based on verbal free association, the dice-rolling leads us back to the girl and the romance at the heart of the film: when one of the losing gamblers steals money from the girl's mother, Charlie uses his "rolling" skills to recover the money, which he restores to her compounded by his own winnings and the interest of his heart.

Once the relationship between Charlie and the girl has been firmly established, Chaplin cuts to the arrival in New York. There is probably no better illustration of how Chaplin's manipulation of our emotions rises above his methods than the frame enlargement (reproduced at the start of this chapter) showing the immigrant, the girl, and her mother looking toward their new home; the fact that the stolid, dolorous woman at the right side of the frame is recognizable as Henry Bergman in drag does nothing to undercut the pathos of the shot or undermine its graphic beauty.

After reducing the entire experience of arriving in America to the mixture of the ideal (seeing the Statue of Liberty) and the real (being treated like cattle while seeing it), Chaplin then jumps with complete narrative abandon to some later point at which Charlie and the girl meet again by chance in a restaurant. In one of his longest comic situations, Chaplin sums up all of the hardships, terrors, and dangers of the immigrant experience in a single question: how is Charlie to escape unharmed after discovering that he has lost his last money and is in danger of being beaten to a pulp by a gang of waiters led by Eric Campbell? The fact that the girl is with him, and that he is feeding her after learning that her mother has died, makes the humor just that much darker and richer. The longest of the individual gags within the restaurant scene—the desparate game Charlie plays to recover a lost coin—parallels the gambling and money games aboard the ship in the first half of the film. Charlie recovers the coin, but it turns out to be as false and transient as most of his dreams. Not until an artist (a comically emotional impressario played by Henry Bergman rather than the romantic type played by Lloyd Bacon) is attracted to the immigrant couple, is there a chance for survival: he offers them a job as models. Significantly, their salvation is not to be found so much in the coin of the realm as in their own personal uniqueness—and in Charlie's ability to make the best of what he finds at hand: he converts the generous tip left by the artist into payment for his own bill.

Lovers offscreen, in *The Immigrant* Chaplin and Edna Purviance play characters who are emotionally closer than ever before, closer because they are both homeless strangers in a new country. Tomorrow they will start their new jobs; tonight they will get married. The decision comes in a studio rain storm that soaks through their dark clothing and makes them gleam like sleek porpoises.

All the glittering prizes were falling into place for Chaplin. On the day *The Immigrant* was released, he signed a new contract worth more than a million dollars. To finish out his Mutual contract, he made *The Adventurer*, a lighthearted comedy in which Charlie escapes from prison, saves Edna and her mother from drowning, competes against the cowardly Eric Campbell for her attention, and escapes from authority at the end by introducing his captor to Edna. When his captor lets go of Charlie to shake Edna's hand, he makes his absurdly easy escape. But Chaplin was about to enter into his longest and most oppressive period of captivity, serving more than five years for what he thought would be an eighteen-month sentence.

2

Journeyman: The First National Films

A Dog's Life

ALTHOUGH MUTUAL offered him a million dollars over and above his production costs to deliver twelve new two-reelers, Chaplin decided to gamble on himself by accepting an offer from the First National film company. In exchange for the delivery of eight two-reelers, Chaplin would receive a minimum of one million dollars—but he would have to pay all production costs. There were two advantages for Chaplin: he would share all profits after the distributors had recovered their costs—and after five years, all rights to the films would revert to him. The disadvantage was that the contract put Chaplin under pressure to make short films quickly when he was driven to make long films slowly. Despite the bind he was now in, it was a better arrangement than the earlier Mutual contract or the new contract Mutual offered because it meant Chaplin would no longer be under pressure to justify his expenditures to the "front office." He escaped internal pressure by refusing to look at cost sheets until each film was completed; he would always rage when he learned how much he spent, said Konrad Bercovici, but his anger was only a game.[1]

Before starting work on his next film, Chaplin bought a five-acre lot on Sunset Boulevard in Hollywood and commissioned construction of the studio where he would make all of his films for the next thirty-five years. Then he sailed to Hawaii with Edna Purviance for a month's rest.

About six months after his last Mutual comedy appeared, his first new film reached the screen in April 1918: A Dog's Life. Generally considered to be Chaplin's first complete masterpiece, it was, at three reels, longer than anything he had directed before.[2] The length results, in part, from the thematic complexity of the "underdog" motif involving three hungry, homeless "mongrels": Charlie, Edna, and Scraps, a dog who foreshadows the scrappy, cast-off boy in The Kid.

The film opens with one of the most realistic images in Chaplin's career. After establishing the dreary slum surroundings, the camera tilts down to reveal Charlie asleep beside a fence full of holes. Resisting being awakened by a draft, he sleepily stuffs a rag in one hole, ignoring others that are larger. The gesture is echoed throughout the film in Charlie's refusal to give in to the apparent hopelessness of any situation—or to make the kind of response the world would consider normal or appropriate. Late in the film, we will see Charlie in his new life as a farmer, planting one seed at a time in a huge field, poking holes in the earth with one finger against the flood waters of hunger and entropy.

To justify the transformation of Charlie from a hungry, cold, homeless, and lonely tramp into a happily married farmer living in a cozy, idyllic cottage, Chaplin creates situations that demonstrate his "worthiness." Though Charlie is initially concerned only with finding food for himself, when he saves the hungry Scraps from a pack of larger dogs he sets in motion a chain of events that eventually leads to his reward. Not content, however, with merely establishing cause and effect relationships to advance the narrative, Chaplin draws early parallels between Charlie and the dog and later between Scraps and Edna. The three are clearly made for each other.

Working together, man and dog manage to feed themselves and then the man goes in search of romance. Constantly faced with the logical problem of how to get a pretty girl like Edna interested in a tramp like Charlie, Chaplin had managed to solve the problem in earlier comedies by having Charlie save Edna from various threats: drowning, Gypsies, hobos, burglars. One of the cleverest solutions was in *Easy Street*: as a missionary, Edna could not only inspire Charlie but could take a legitimate interest in his future. In all of these earlier comedies, with the exception of the obligatory equality of the immigrants two films earlier, Edna had been on a higher social, moral or economic plane than Charlie. Now, as a cabaret singer in a den of thieves, she is just as much an underdog as Charlie and Scraps.

Edna and Charlie meet in *A Dog's Life* because her boss orders her to flirt with the customers after she finishes singing. This narrative gimmick establishes the danger of sexual exploitation facing Edna and provides a wonderful opportunity for comedy: the innocent girl's attempts to flirt make her look demented or neurologically defective. Always a gentleman, Charlie does her the courtesy of thinking she has something in her eye—and she proves herself worthy of this courtesy by quitting her job rather than do more than sing.

The three central characters and their search for food and love come together in the middle of the film after Scraps, who is digging for a bone, finds a stolen wallet. This discovery precipitates one of Chaplin's most brilliant pantomime sequences (Charlie must make his hands seem to be the hands of an unconscious ruffian seated at a table in the cabaret) and leads to the "when dreams come true" ending: Charlie and Edna use the contents of the wallet to get married and buy a farm. In the final scene, Chaplin reinforces the connections between the humans and the dog: as Charlie and Edna look down into a bassinet, the camera tilts to reveal the fruit of their union, Scraps and her litter of puppies. After they kiss one of the puppies, Charlie raises his eyebrows in comic resignation.

A Dog's Life represents a tremendous change in direction for Chaplin, a totally new departure. The most obvious reason for this change is that with the switch from Mutual, Chaplin had to build a new repertory company. Leo White, the veteran of twenty earlier Chaplin films, was gone, and so were Frank Coleman, Charlotte Mineau, and Lloyd Bacon, Charlie's frequent rival or alter ego. The most significant loss was Eric Campbell, who had been killed in an auto accident late in 1917. More than anything else, the loss of the massively villainous and talented Campbell was responsible for the change in direction. With Campbell, Chaplin would have probably been tempted to repeat and emphasize the constant David and Goliath conflict of the Mutual comedies; without him, Chaplin was able to cut back on the amount of comedy built around their differences in size. Until Chaplin brought in Mack Swain for the last three of the First National films, a tall, bland, big-boned actor named Tom Wilson replaced Campbell in function—but not in form or ferocity—as the menacing cop in *A Dog's Life* and *The Kid*, the drill sergeant in *Shoulder Arms*, the boss in *Sunnyside*, and the jealous husband Charlie fights in *A Day's Pleasure*. At the outset of the First National period, then, there were only two constants: Edna would be the heroine and Chaplin would contrive his plots through what he called the simple "process of getting people in and out of trouble" (A, 211).

Shoulder Arms

War had broken out in Europe during Chaplin's first year in the movies. By the time he finished *A Dog's Life*, America had entered the war and Chaplin, with the two other reigning monarchs of Hollywood, Douglas Fairbanks and Mary Pickford, officiated at the opening of the third Liberty Bond campaign and went on tour. As a result of seeing the martial fervor around the country, he decided to put Charlie in uniform and began *Shoulder Arms* in spite of warnings that it would be danger- ous to make fun of the war. Lewis Jacobs, one of the earliest film historians, calls *Shoulder Arms* a "contribution to America's war chest" and asserts that Charlie's repudiation of "his peaceful ideals" by joining the army is a "suggestion for others to do likewise."[3] Such a reading mistakenly posits "peaceful ideals" in a figure who is constantly making war on those who need to have war made on them. As to the suggestion the film is a recruiting poster, we need only consider that it was made in the last months of the war and released less than a month before the Armistice—and that it reduces the war to an opportunity for comedy and parodies the conventions of the war movies of the time by mocking heroism and turning the cruel Huns into cartoon figures.

What is most interesting about *Shoulder Arms* is not its place in the social history of its times, but in Chaplin's career and the development of his concept of his screen persona. Chaplin claims that he planned for *Shoulder Arms* to be his first feature, a five-reeler moving from Charlie's home life and induction through his basic training and experiences at the front, culminating with a banquet "showing all the crowned heads of Europe celebrating my heroic act of capturing the Kaiser." The banqueting was never photographed, but Chaplin did shoot the opening scenes in which tippling Charlie is shown with four children, the offspring of a frying-pan wielding wife who is never seen, her size only suggested by an "enormous chemise . . . hanging on the kitchen line." This Maggie and Jiggs vision of marriage was followed by an induction sequence for which Chaplin shot a series of gags built around Charlie's fear of being seen naked by female clerks. Chaplin shelved these two opening sequences because "I thought it better to keep Charlot a nondescript with no background and to discover him already in the army" (A, 220).

Although he discarded two reels of expensive footage to keep the "purity" of the character, Chaplin retained the short and rather routine stateside drill sequence in order to establish a dream framework for Charlie's adventures on the battlefield. After drilling as the most inept member of the "awkward squad," Private Charlie falls asleep and dreams that he is in the trenches. The first part of that dream is among the best things Chaplin did. In spite of one pantomime that looks like an updated Karno routine (Chaplin and his brother Sydney mime watching an enemy plane crash at the end of a long "turn" about Charlie as an Olympic-quality sniper), it is an epic display of the ability of Charlie and Chaplin to get "inside" a new environment and transform it for their own purposes: Charlie holds up a bottle to be opened by a passing bullet, mistakes explosions behind him for his own flatulent eruptions, turns an overripe cheese into a smelly bomb, adapts to a flooded bunker, and becomes part of the landscape by disguising himself as a tree.

If the first part of Charlie's tour of duty at the front is a brilliantly disarming tour de force, the second part is simply forced. Edna Purviance is introduced as an embodiment of "Poor France" in a liberty cap. Like her country, and like the "Goddess of Liberty" Purviance plays in

The Bond, a half-reel of propaganda vignettes Chaplin made for the Liberty Loan Appeal, she must be saved by Charlie from the lecherous, rape-minded Huns. Jarringly inconsistent with the sentimentalized personification of *la belle France* is the rather cavalier way both Chaplin and Charlie treat her: the sly character manages to keep his hand on her knee while pretending to be asleep—and the artist exploits the French girl as an opportunity for a sexual joke (when the Kaiser finds Charlie putting on a German uniform to disguise himself, he winkingly assumes that Charlie is getting dressed after sexual dalliance with the girl in his office). In short, the attitude toward the girl is casual and completely lacking in the elements of romance, emotion, and sacrifice Chaplin employed with such great effect in *The Tramp, The Vagabond, Easy Street,* and *The Immigrant.*

Trouble in Paradise

If 1916 was Chaplin's best, most satisfying year, 1919 was its opposite, a dreadful, dreary year in which he released two of his least pleasant films, *Sunnyside* and *A Day's Pleasure.* The first is definitely not sunny; the second gives pleasure a bad name and reduces it to the transience of a single day. Part of the problem was that the contract with First National became burdensome when Chaplin formed United Artists with three of the most important and popular film artists of the time: D. W. Griffith, Douglas Fairbanks, and Mary Pickford. This new distribution company needed features from Chaplin, and Chaplin—whose recent films had been longer and more sophisticated in their narrative structure—wanted to make features. But he still had to make six more short films to fulfill his eight picture contract with First National.

Even more onerous was the other contract he had entered into late in 1918 when he married Mildred Harris, a teen-aged actress (most sources say she was sixteen), after she claimed to have become pregnant by him. Even serious critics, confronting the folly of Chaplin's marriage to an untalented girl who grew up to become an alcoholic night-club performer, reduce themselves to the level of fan-club gossip by asking why Chaplin did not marry Edna Purviance. Chaplin evades the question himself, implying Edna was somehow to blame because of her interest in a handsome leading man. He admits that "at the back of my mind" was the idea he might one day marry her. "But I had reservations about Edna. I was uncertain of her, and for that matter uncertain of myself" (*A,* 204). Raoul Sobel and David Francis indirectly give us what seems the best answer to the question: "His ideal woman might possibly have been one who was mature and accommodating toward his moods and obsessions, a mistress and mother substitute at the same time. But maturity was not something Chaplin could readily face. It betokened control, caution, a sense of proportion and a knowledge of the rules of the game."[4] Edna Purviance, then in her mid-twenties, approached the ideal described by Sobel and Francis: she knew his moods and she knew the rules.

As we will see, Chaplin blames his first marriage for the failure of *Sunnyside*, a false pastoral remembered today primarily for the graceful and poetic "ballet" in which Charlie hallucinates or dreams that he is dancing like Pan with four gauze-draped nymphs. Highly pictorial in its composition, lighting, and choreography, *Sunnyside* is emotionally unsettling because Chaplin has extended the fairy-tale ending of *A Dog's Life* into an entire film. The effect is overwhelmingly, nightmarishly surrealistic—Charlie is awakened at the start into the world of the Hotel Evergreen, a country inn where he cuts the grass that grows in the lobby, puts a hen in a frying pan to lay his breakfast egg, and brings in a whole cow to put cream in his tea. Near the end, despairing the loss of Edna to a handsome city slicker, he throws himself in front of a speeding car and is awakened yet again by a kick from the boss who awakened him in the morning. The film ends with Charlie and Edna hugging and dancing in a transport of delight that seems no more realistic than those dream fantasies.

The character played by Edna Purviance—a homely, none-too-bright farmer's daughter—is so strange, so unreal, that it is tempting to turn to *My Autobiography* for evidence that she is a projection of Chaplin's bride: "to Mildred marriage was an adventure as thrilling as winning a beauty contest. It was something she had read about in storybooks. She had no sense of reality. . . . She was in a continual state of dazzlement" (A, 230); "her mind. . . . was cluttered with pink-ribboned foolishness. She seemed in a dither, looking always for other horizons" (A, 239). Much of Chaplin's bitterness toward his first wife grew out of his anger over her signing of a contract with Louis B. Mayer, who planned to bill her in movies as "Mrs. Charlie Chaplin." Compare the silly country girl in *Sunnyside* who falls prey to the solicitations of a flashy outsider.

Early in *Sunnyside*, Chaplin had inserted an intertitle to introduce the girl: "And now the romance." In his next film, Chaplin put aside all thought of romance and opened with the conceit that Charlie and Edna are married and that they have a pair of sons who, like little clones, wear juvenile variations of the "costume." Outside of the costume joke, however, the kids have no point in the film. Like the wife, they are entirely passive and supply no opportunity for pathos or humor—and Charlie seems barely aware of their presence. Quite literally, they are along for the ride, first in the family's Model T, later on an excursion boat. In a fairly typical scene, the wife and children sleep in deck chairs

while Charlie struggles to open one for himself; in another, the children
sleep on while big Tom Wilson tries to strangle their daddy. Charlie and
Edna join other couples in a joyless dance on the rocking deck, but
Charlie soon feels queazy and goes off by himself. In sum, Charlie is no
more affectionate a husband than—if Mildred Harris's heavily pub-
licized complaints can be credited—Chaplin himself.

Denis Gifford suggests that *A Day's Pleasure* was an attempt to forget
his unhappy marriage by creating "life as he wanted it to be,"[5] but it is
hard to see why anyone would want the kind of life depicted here.
Except for one transcendent, gravity-defying moment in which Charlie,
stuck in tar, bobs and sways back and forth beyond the grasp of a fat cop,
it is an ugly life full of dull frustrations (the car that will not start, the
folding chair that will not unfold, the traffic jam), cruel jokes about
blacks, repetitive attention to seasickness, and casual violence culminating in two outbursts by Charlie: first he kicks a pesky child trying to sell
him buttered popcorn, then he beats up the gigantic but helplessly
seasick Tom Wilson, punching him repeatedly in the groin shortly
before the final ironic intertitle: "The end of a perfect day."[6]

More misogynistic (if not misogamistic) than any other Chaplin film, *A
Day's Pleasure* unveils as unpleasant a view of the relations between men
and women as is to be found in James Thurber's cartoons. A very large
woman with a very small husband blocks traffic as she gossips in the
middle of the street; after another large woman sprawls between the pier
and the excursion boat, Charlie first uses her backside as a gang plank to
run aboard, then considers hauling her to safety with a lethal-looking
gaffing hook; the final battle is precipitated by what an intertitle calls "a
forced acquaintance" between Charlie and another man's wife. Nearly
sixty years later, the persistence of Chaplin's resentment of his own
"forced acquaintance" with Mildred Harris is revealed in *My Life in
Pictures* by the photograph he chose to represent himself at the time of
his marriage. It shows him collarless, unkempt, unshaven, and with
deep wrinkles: "Here we look like Beauty and the Beast. I hate this
picture of me. I look bleary-eyed, like a murderer. No wonder!" (*ML*,
177).

Significantly, *A Day's Pleasure* is the only First National film not
mentioned in *My Autobiography*. Chaplin seems to have forgotten or
repressed it in his rush to get from the disaster of *Sunnyside* to the
triumph of *The Kid*. Consider the passage in which he jumps from
complaints about Mildred Harris to his "discovery" of Jackie Coogan:
"After we were married Mildred's pregnancy turned out to be a false
alarm. Several months had passed and I had completed only a three-reel
comedy, *Sunnyside,* and that had been like pulling teeth. Without
question marriage was having an effect on my creative faculties. After

Sunnyside I was at my wits' end for an idea. It was a relief in this state of despair to go to the Orpheum for distraction, and in this state of mind I saw . . . an infant of four" (*A*, 231). What is particularly interesting and revealing about this passage is that Chaplin has avoided a full accounting of the reasons for his "state of despair." The pieces of the puzzle begin to fall together when we turn to *My Life in Pictures*, where he devotes two pages to samples of the production reports and cutting continuity "for the film that was finally released as *A Day's Pleasure*" (*ML*, 182–83). On the report for Thursday, 10 July, we learn that "Charlie's Picnic" had been in production for a total of forty-three days, of which thirty-four had been idle. At the bottom is a simple notation: "Did Not Shoot. Norman Spencer Chaplin passed on today." The obituary reference is to the apparent source of Chaplin's despair, the deformed infant born three days before. At the bottom of the same page, he reproduces a pair of production reports for something called "The Ford Story." Whereas it had taken forty-three days to shoot a total of sixty-five hundred feet of film for "Charlie's Picnic," it took only twelve days, of which only four were idle, to shoot over twenty-five thousand feet for "The Ford Story," which became *A Day's Pleasure*. A close reading of the production reports for "The Ford Story" reveals three things: it involved a boat, most of it was shot nonstop in a six-day period, and Jackie Coogan was in it. The last was the most important, for Chaplin wanted Coogan to get used to the cameras before starting the picture that was slowly forming in his mind, *The Kid*.

The "Playful Pain" of *The Kid*

Speaking of *A Day's Pleasure* in a recent interview, Jackie Coogan claimed Chaplin "kind of sloughed that picture off."[7] The speed of the production, the way some shots seem to last too long (Chaplin uses up nearly half a minute to show people disembarking from the boat at the end), the fact that it is the shortest of all his two-reelers, and its general dullness and apathy, all support Coogan's memory and suggest Chaplin was holding himself under tight control in order to finish something, anything, to chip away at the First National contract and keep himself before the public at a time when rivals were grinding out comedies at a much faster pace. But except for press reports of his marital troubles and the divorce suit charging him with mental cruelty, Chaplin disappeared from the public eye in 1920, the first year since his film debut that he did not release a single new film. For a while, it may have looked as though there was some truth in the recent prediction of an "expert" that, "in the natural course of events, the Chaplin vogue in five years will be a thing of remote antiquity."[8] But in 1921 the explosion of popular and critical adulation for *The Kid* would seem even more brilliant against the gloom and failure of the two previous years.

Max Eastman, who lived with Chaplin during the making of *The Kid* and had long talks with him about comedy because he was writing a book on the subject, ends the first part of *The Sense of Humor* with a comment (on J. M. Barrie's *Sentimental Tommy*) that could be applied to many scenes in *The Kid* and most of the Chaplin features that followed: "That was one of those trembling moments . . . of which we say, 'I did not know whether to laugh or cry!' They reveal to us better than any discourse can what humor is, and why it is. . . . Humor is a most adroit and exquisite device by which our nerves outwit the stings and paltry business of life."[9] Chaplin himself alludes to Eastman's theory in *My Autobiography*, saying that Eastman sums up humor "as being derived from playful pain. He writes that Homo sapiens is masochistic, enjoying pain in many forms and that the audience likes to suffer vicariously. . . . With all this I agree. But. . . ." Where Chaplin differs from Eastman is that he values the "playful pain" of humor because it "heightens our sense of survival and preserves our sanity. Because of humor we are less overwhelmed by the vicissitudes of life. It activates our sense of proportion and reveals to us that in an overstatement of seriousness lurks the absurd" (*A*, 211–12).

The Kid opens with a title card that promises Eastman's "trembling moments" to come: "A picture with a smile—and perhaps, a tear." And then comes the "overstatement of seriousness" in which lurks the absurd, the melodramatic scenes involving the Woman (Edna Purviance)—scenes that Chaplin himself calls "slow and solemn" (*A*, 242). We should try to put ourselves in the place of the original audience, and imagine the uncertainty of watching a Chaplin film that goes on for long minute after minute without any sign of Charlie or a smile. First, we see a prisonlike charity hospital, from which comes the nameless Woman "whose sin was motherhood," then the sudden frozen image of Christ bearing a cross in hazy counterpoint to the Woman and her infant burden, then the gratuitous intertitle informing us the Woman is "Alone" when we can see that for ourselves. By the time Chaplin introduces "The Man," a handsome artist in a romantically Bohemian studio, it becomes even more difficult to tell whether he is playing it straight or parodying screen melodramas like Griffith's *Way Down East*. The "artistic" chiaroscuro of the "Rembrandt lighting" in the Man's studio seems to be unquestionably romantic, but what are we to make of the incident in which he accidentally knocks the Woman's picture into the fire, plucks it out, sees that it is scorched, and throws it back? The symbolic point is clear enough: she is spoiled goods to be consigned to the flames—but the casual way in which the artist lights his pipe from those flames leaves us uneasy about whether or not we are to laugh. The emotional intent is still murky when the Woman puts the infant in the back of a limousine parked in front of a mansion, but the light begins to break when two stereotypical thugs, moving with the jerkiness of under-cranked comic figures, steal the limousine. Their startled reaction to the noise in the back seat, the way one thug pulls a gun, their disgust at finding the baby, all prepare us for other surprises to come. Chaplin then signals an end to the melodramatic prologue with two matched iris-outs: in one, the stolen limousine speeds away from us after the thugs abandon the baby in an alley; in the other, the Woman walks slowly away as the darkness closes slowly around her. When the iris opens to reveal Charlie sauntering up the alley toward the camera, we can let out our breath: Charlie's in the picture, all's right with the world, and it's time to laugh, for that whole bathetic opening has been building carefully and cleverly toward an epic comic reversal: the Woman wants her child to have the best in life—and the Kid ends up in the care of Charlie.

Initially, however, Charlie does not want the baby. To him, it seems just another bit of the garbage he has been trying to avoid ever since he walked into frame. First, he is almost hit by garbage thrown down from an upper story. Then, as he gets closer to the camera, a second pile of garbage hits him squarely from above. Although he is constantly "dumped" on, Charlie does not seem to mind, for he matter-of-factly inspects the garbage that just rained down to see if it is of any use to him, then opens his sardine can "cigarette case" to select a smoke from an assortment of butts. These gestures suggest that he "lives" on garbage, at least to the extent of relying on it for his simple pleasures. Not until this point is established does Chaplin have Charlie notice the baby that will become his chief pleasure; assuming it is garbage, he looks up to see where it might have been dropped from.

After trying to unload the baby three times, Charlie still refuses to accept the responsibility. He sits down on the curb, opens a sewer grate, looks at the baby, back at the sewer opening, shakes his head, and closes the grate. The baby may be human garbage, but it does not deserve to become sewage. Only now is Chaplin ready for Charlie to discover the note pinned to the baby: "Please love and care for this orphan child." For a long beat, he looks noncommittally at the child, then breaks into a huge smile. In that instant, all the little acts of kindness exhibited by past Charlies toward past Ednas in two dozen movies, acts inspired by his attraction to her feminine beauty, have blossomed into his first "pure" act of kindness toward another human—the first act, that is, untainted by any hint of sexual or romantic attraction. Chaplin, who had married in haste, who had seen his first-born die, had now chosen to make a film about Charlie accepting responsibility for feeding, clothing, sheltering, rearing, and loving someone else's little bastard.

When Charlie stands up to walk away from us, the camera remains fixed—a touch of such great psychological subtlety that we might mistake it for a flaw rather than a visual metaphor for the way Charlie and Chaplin have risen above the mere mechanics of the film and the plot, have ascended out of the common frame, leaving behind the pavement, the gutter, the sewer, and all mortal baseness.

Charlie's acceptance of the Kid comes near the end of the first reel in this six-reeler. After that one brief instant in which Charlie's face registers his heart's response, Chaplin will milk the relationship between Charlie and the Kid for laughs until near the end of the fourth reel, when the child is taken away from him. The strategy is clear: he wants to delay as long as possible the inevitable moment when Charlie's feelings for the Kid, and the audience's perception of those feelings, will explode unbearably. For that reason, he puts the emotional burden on the unwed mother early in the film and has Edna Purviance discharge it conventionally as the fallen woman of stage and screen melodrama. Thus, the scene in which she has a change of heart and returns to the place where she left the baby, only to find that the limousine and baby have been stolen, results in obligatory screaming and fainting (and, presumably, the first step on the road to her moral regeneration)—and sets up the cut back to Charlie, who makes us forget about the hysterical mother by demonstrating, in less than two minutes, his ability to transform his shabby surroundings into a nursery.[10] The scene is short but masterful: the suckling is cradled in a kind of hammock below a dangling coffee pot while Charlie turns old sheets into new diapers. Then, planning ahead, he cuts a hole in the bottom of a chair and places this makeshift potty chair over a spittoon as the scene fades out.

In a blink of the eye, it is five years later and the house-broken Kid is an urchin sitting on the curb. He goes inside for his morning inspection by Papa Charlie, a model of fastidiousness in spite of his shabby garb and surroundings. And then they go to work, the Kid breaking windows and Charlie repairing them. This "occupation" is a wonderful summary of the fragility of the existence led by Charlie and the Kid: they live off their environment, the one creating a need, the other supplying a service. But there is also danger, for the Kid gets caught with a rock by a big cop who then goes home to find Charlie flirting with his good-natured wife. Thus does Chaplin connect the breaking of windows by which they survive with the breaking of rules that led to the birth of the Kid. Never before had Chaplin treated the life-and-death consequences of sexual attraction with as much seriousness as he does here. It is funny when the jealous cop reaches through the broken window to choke Charlie, but it is not quite as funny when Charlie dreams that the same cop shoots him after a fracas that results from another flirtation. It is difficult not to conclude that this paradoxically darker and yet more joyous vision of the consequences of passion is a result of the maturity thrust upon Chaplin by the emotional and marital shocks of the year that preceded the start of *The Kid.*

Having shown how Charlie and the Kid make their living, Chaplin now shows their return to the garret room where their supper has been cooking. As Charlie piles a huge mound of potatoes and vegetables on the Kid's plate, we cut to the Woman, who has somehow managed to become a prominent opera star. Enter to her a walking tower of floral tribute, a huge display of roses carried by a little delivery boy who is almost as cute as the Kid. She smiles fondly at him, tips him generously, and prepares to go out as we cut back to Charlie and the Kid finishing their supper. As the Kid prepares to go outside to play, we cut to the street where the Woman is dispensing charity to a poor mother with a baby. Holding the baby, the Woman nearly swoons, presumably at the memory of her own child—but when she turns and sees the Kid, she simply smiles at him, just as she smiled at the cute delivery boy a few minutes before. Her response to the baby is melodramatic; it is the audience that makes the melodramatic response when she sees the Kid, crying out for the Woman to know her son. She gives him a toy dog and a ball, then walks away as the Kid waves after her.

Now, less than two minutes after the end of the supper scene, Chaplin inserts a second meal that calls attention to itself through its proximity to and differences from the first. It is a pancake breakfast prepared and served by the Kid while Charlie reads in bed. The Kid has become a surrogate mother for Charlie and Chaplin. Just as the room in which the scene takes place "was based to a large extent on the places in Lambeth and Kennington where Sydney and I had lived with our mother when we were children" (*ML*, 188), the action and mood of the scene are a nostalgic evocation of the life he led with his mother, who could "make that miserable garret glow with golden comfort" (*A*, 12). He remembers especially those wintry Sundays "when she would give me my breakfast in bed and I would awaken to a tidy little room with a small fire glowing and see the steaming kettle on the hob and a haddock or a bloater by the fender being kept warm while she made toast. Mother's cheery presence, the coziness of the room, the soft padded sound of boiling water pouring into our earthenware teapot while I read my weekly comic, were the pleasures of a serene Sunday morning." The psychological implications become even more complex when we realize that if the Kid is a miniature version of Charlie, then the Woman is also a surrogate mother to Charlie, the alter ego of Chaplin who was just then making arrangements to bring his own "long-lost" mother to America.

The breakfast scene ends the five-year idyll of Charlie and the Kid; the remaining garret scenes will be interrupted by outsiders who will attempt to separate the two. But before we go on to the painful pleasures of the second half of *The Kid*, let us first pay attention to the very end of the breakfast scene, which comes almost exactly at the midpoint in the film. Charlie is sated, bored, indifferent, sucking his teeth, totally unaware that his world is about to change as the Kid holds up his toy dog to be kissed. At this point, we have not seen Charlie kiss the Kid; in fact, Charlie seems emotionally unresponsive to the Kid, a point made lightly at the end of the morning toilette scene: when the Kid kisses him, Charlie shoves the boy away with his foot. Thus, the toy dog, a present from the Woman, serves to project the Kid's need for something more than the food, shelter, clothing, discipline, and street smarts supplied by Charlie.

The toy dog, which is replaced by an angelic puppy in the final dream sequence, also connects *The Kid* to *A Dog's Life*, the Coogan character to Scraps. The similarities seem to have been intentional, for Chaplin posed for a still showing him sitting with Coogan in a pose similar to an earlier publicity still with Scraps. The complex symbolic and narrative "payoff" of the Kid/Scraps connection begins when a neighborhood bully takes the toy dog away from the Kid, precipitating the fight that leads to the final action. After the scrappy Kid licks his bigger antagonist, he suddenly becomes sick. The Woman, who gave the Kid the toy that became the bone of contention, now tells Charlie the Kid needs a doctor. This in turn leads directly to another parallel between Scraps and the Kid, and between the Kid and Charlie, for just as the little bully took the toy Scraps away from the Kid, the Kid is taken away from Charlie by three officials.

Trapped between two larger men, Charlie must listen helplessly as the Kid screams and begs not to be taken away. After turning all human relations into gags, Chaplin suddenly, shockingly hits us with a dual display of emotion: the tearful and tear-jerking screams of the Kid, and the stricken eyes of the frantic Charlie. Reunited in the back of the truck from the orphanage, Charlie hugs the Kid and kisses him full on the mouth in undisguised and unequaled emotion. From that point on, Charlie will repeatedly kiss the Kid without hesitation.

Everything that follows this moment of unconditional surrender to the dictates of the heart is anticlimactic, an elaborate working-out of the terms of the inevitable reunion of the Woman and her lost son. For that reason, as soon as Charlie has saved the Kid from "social" authority, Chaplin shows the Woman, the "natural" authority, reading the note she left with the infant five years before. Chaplin then returns us to Charlie, the Kid, and the highest authority known to the motion pictures, the emotional. The setting is a flophouse with a prominently displayed sign: "Management not *responsible* for VALUABLES STOLEN." This portentous warning is followed by a comic pantomime involving a pickpocket (Jack Coogan, Jackie's father) who inadvertently helps Charlie discover resources he did not know he had: in one of Charlie's many pockets, the thief finds a lost or forgotten coin betokening, perhaps, the buried or unknown feelings of love unleashed earlier by the theft of the child. This serendipitous coin, which Charlie has the Kid kiss goodby, is the price extracted for the admission of the Kid to the flophouse by the stolid, Dickensian manager who moments later turns out the light and "steals" the Kid from Charlie.

Now Charlie is thrust into a waking nightmare in which he searches the dark and mean streets and sets left over from *A Dog's Life*. This waking nightmare passage will be followed by the much-maligned dream sequence, but not before the dawn reunion of mother and child at the police station, a reunion that is necessary to right the first wrong. Ignored by Chaplin's critics, this first reunion is, like the scene in which Charlie decides to keep the infant rather than drop it down the sewer, a masterful use of understatement. Gone are the Woman's earlier histrionics: she does no more than smile at the Kid and dab at her eyes. Chaplin forces the audience to supply the emotion by having the Kid remain expressionless as his mother smiles at him—and by having her envelop him in her arms, hiding his face from view with her hair and her fur coat, thus creating a private environment for whatever revelations, tears, or smiles they share.

With the fade-out on the reunion of mother and child, Chaplin is ready for the dream of "heaven" from which Charlie will be awakened to the only paradise he can ever know, that of the real world. Though mistakenly criticized as an irrelevant sugar-plum concoction, the dream is an intentionally stagy and old-fashioned fantasy of a false paradise tainted by sin and death. The charge that the dream is irrelevant or pointless is easily dismissed, for the dream recycles the experiences of Charlie in a simple style and imagery appropriate to the limited imagination of the dreamer. Chaplin seems to have borrowed this technique from a 1916 J. M. Barrie play, *A Kiss for Cinderella*, in which a poor girl's dream of a palace ball is described as being "not as balls are, but as they are conceived to be in a little chamber in Cinderella's head."[11] Reviewing *The Kid* for the *New Republic*, Francis Hackett saw the dream for what it was, "A simple man's version of the Big Change, made up from the few properties with which a simple man would be likely to acquainted. The lack of inventiveness seemed to me to be its best point."[12]

Charlie dreams that his neighborhood and neighbors have been transformed, the buildings painted white and garlanded with flowers, the citizens turned into angels. Though the Kid comes to Charlie at the start of the dream, Charlie soon ignores the Kid and turns all of his attention to a little female angel who seems to come from some remote little chamber in the mind of Chaplin rather than of Charlie. Just as the Kid replaces the Edna character as a focus for Charlie's affections, now the flirtatious angel replaces the Kid. The bad little angel also "replaces" the basic Edna character and prefigures Chaplin's "post-Purviance" heroines, the dark little gamines in *Modern Times* and *The Great Dictator*, the dance hall girl (that is, prostitute) in *The Gold Rush*, the bare back rider in *The Circus*, the blind girl who plies her trade on street corners in *City Lights*, the prostitute in *Monsieur Verdoux*, and the ballerina in *Limelight* who is at first thought to be a streetwalker by Calvero. Thus, the bad angel within the dream seems to grow out of Chaplin's efforts to find his way in his career by asking the question, "Now that Charlie has lost the Kid who was a replacement for Edna, what next?"

It is an ominous fact that during the last stage of shooting *The Kid*, Chaplin expanded the role of the angelic vamp and gave Edna Purviance's dressing room to Lillita McMurray, the twelve-year-old girl who played the part. Four years later, having "retired" Edna (the actress and the character), Chaplin hired the same girl to play the female lead in *The Gold Rush*. But as in the dream sequence, where "sin creeps in," Chaplin's life would intrude upon his art: the girl became pregnant and was transformed from leading lady to wife, from romantic ideal to inconveniently real.

In Barrie's *A Kiss for Cinderella*, an oversized London "Bobby" awakens the heroine in order to spirit her away to a better life in the real world. Here, after being shot down by the angelic cop because of the fracas over the angelic flirt, the dead Charlie of the dream dissolves to the real Charlie being awakened by the real cop (played by the same actor, Tom Wilson, who shook him from his dreams in *Sunnyside* and *Shoulder Arms*). Chaplin now reverses the limousine trip that brought the Kid to Charlie by having another limousine bring Charlie to the Kid. At the door of the Woman's mansion, Charlie is reunited with the Kid, and the cop who has been his constant nemesis both awake and dreaming now shakes his hand and pats his shoulder. Charlie enters the mansion and, in reversal of the opening of the door to the maternity hospital at the start, the door closes behind him.

Though the formal circularity of the film made it unnecessary for Chaplin to supply any hint of what will come beyond the closing of that second door, there were objections about the ambiguous or indeterminate nature of the ending. Such objections are actually misplaced complaints about the entire narrative and emotional strategy. Chaplin could have established bonds of attraction between Charlie and the Woman; by making her a famous opera star (rather than, say, a hired girl like the seduced and abandoned heroine of Griffith's *Way Down East*), he has put her on a pedestal so that romance would not and could not be an issue. As we will see, the distance he imposes between the Woman and Charlie is symptomatic of the formal separation that eventually led to the professional divorce of Chaplin and Purviance.

Seems Like Old Times: *The Idle Class*

Once the shooting of *The Kid* was complete, Chaplin found himself in the same position as Charlie: the film itself had become, like the Kid, the center of a custody dispute. Suspecting that his wife's lawyers were planning to attach the unedited film as community property, he did what many parents of human offspring do under similar circumstances: he fled the state with his brain child. After cutting the film, he cut an attractive financial deal with First National: they would advance him one and a half million dollars for the right to distribute *The Kid* for five years and 50 percent of the profits. There was only one drawback: the six reels of *The Kid* would not count toward completion of the eight picture contract. He still had four short pictures to go before he would be able to start producing features as an independent and releasing them through United Artists. Partly because of the high standards he would expect of himself after the success of *The Kid* (the public loved it and the critics were almost universally favorable, some calling it a classic, sublime, Dickensian, and a work of genius), it would take him nearly two years to complete the contract.

After being lionized by artists, literati, and the money elite during a long vacation in New York and Long Island just before and after the release of *The Kid* in February of 1921, Chaplin returned to California to begin *The Idle Class*, a film that explores more intensely than any other the split between his person and his persona. The millionaire Chaplin plays the rich Mr. Charles (the name appears in a telegram) as well as the raggedly familiar Charlie, who arrives at a winter resort of the idle class by train. But whereas the bored, effete members of the idle class climb down from their first class coaches, Charlie crawls out from under the train with his carpet bag and golf clubs. The conceit is superb: Charlie is the underclass of the idle class, the id beneath the ego of Mr. Charles.

Late in the film, Mr. Charles is trapped inside a suit of armor, his identity hidden until Charlie releases his double by pulling out a can opener and peeling back the mask.

Chaplin, like Mr. Charles, was a guest at his own masquerade. In the next few years, rumors would surface about Chaplin wanting to play Napoleon and Christ, but except for the comically surrealistic double identities in *The Great Dictator*, it would be more than a quarter century before he abandoned entirely Charlie or his costume for the role of Monsieur Verdoux, a murderous character of many identities.

In addition to exploring the specific nature of his screen identity in *The Idle Class*, Chaplin also toyed with the nature of his on-screen relationship to the Edna character. In what seems a cruel reference to the fact she had started drinking heavily during the making of *The Kid*, Edna Purviance plays a wife who feels she is neglected because her husband drinks too much. Though she looks very elegant when she steps down from the train at the start of the film, she also looks quite heavy, expressionless, bovine. By the end of the film, in her Madame Pompadour costume and constant pout, she looks unattractive and more than slightly ridiculous.

To the cruelty of the casting and costuming, Chaplin adds Charlie's lukewarm response to Edna. At first, he is sufficiently attracted to daydream about her, but the fantasized images of courtship, marriage, and a baby are so conventional and speed by so quickly that romance becomes a hit and run victim. Later, when he is mistaken for Edna's husband at a masked ball, he instantly denies the honor. Finally, when he is ordered from Edna's presence by her father, he looks no more than mildly disappointed, as though he has been outbid at an auction for an attractive knicknack he would like to possess but can live without. Charlie's brief last glance at Edna is foreshadowed by his rich doppelgänger's response to her note that she intends to live apart until he stops drinking: he picks up her photograph, looks at it, puts it down, hunches his shoulders with his back to us, and seems to weep convulsively—but when he turns around, we see that he is merely agitating a cocktail shaker. And when her father, at Edna's insistence, comes to apologize to him, Charlie accepts the apology, then kicks the older man's butt and runs off into the distance. So much for romance and pathos: Chaplin would rather give the audience the "classic" image of ink-blot Chaplin disappearing up the whiteness of the sidewalk as an iris closes on the happy-go-lucky trickster of the earlier comedies.

Indeed, after the moral and emotional complexities of *The Kid*, Chaplin seems to have been trying to fall back on the simpler effects of his earlier films. Avoiding any attempts at pathos or serious intent, he recycles gags and situations we have seen before, combining Sennett madness and ass-kicking with the elaborate sets and the "environmental" humor of the Mutual period. And there is, surely, nostalgia in his casting of big Mack Swain as his nemesis on the golf links and as the father of Edna. Acting with Swain must have brought back memories of Keystone, where they had acted together, but there is also nostalgia for the Mutual days in Swain's makeup. The beard and preposterously slanted eyebrows are so similar to Eric Campbell's typical "Mikado" makeup that even Chaplin was fooled: in *My Autobiography* he identifies a photograph of Swain as "Eric Campbell in *The Idle Class*" (*A*, 263).

The Idle Class is the same kind of elegant but emotionally dead tour de force as the parody of the death scene in *Camille* that he played for guests at a party at about the same time: "As she was dying in my arms, she started coughing, slightly at first, then with increasing momentum. Her coughing became so infectious that I caught it from her. Then it became a coughing contest between us. Eventually it was I who did the dying in Camille's arms" (*A*, 264). Granted, the conceit is amusing, but parody (or self-parody) was something that Chaplin turned to when he was overworked, when he could not solve the human problems of motivation. Thus with the film he began after spending his talents on *The Idle Class*. It was to be "a burlesque on the prosperous occupation of plumbers" and would open with a joke about Charlie and his partner arriving in a chauffeured limousine to make a house call on Edna's sick bathroom. "This was as far as I got," Chaplin writes. "I could concentrate no further. I did not realize how tired I was" (*A*, 263). Shelving the plumber movie, he closed his studio and went "home" to England in the grand style aboard the same ship on which he had come to America nine years before as an unknown passenger down in second class.

"Who Am I?"—*My Trip Abroad* and *The Pilgrim*

The voyage home and the triumphal tour of England and Europe brought to an end the first major stage in Chaplin's career. Only a month and a half in duration, the trip was an emotionally charged pilgrimage in which Chaplin revisited the scenes of his youth, learned that Hetty Kelly (the object of his adolescent infatuation) was dead, and met some of the writers and dramatists he most admired, including George Bernard Shaw, J. M. Barrie, H. G. Wells, and Thomas Burke.

On the train back to California from New York, Chaplin dictated his adventures for publication as *My Trip Abroad*. Thomas Burke was impressed by this little book, predicting that "Fifty years hence, it will, I think, be re-discovered . . . and it may then take its place as one of the complete and natural pieces of self-revelation.[13] More than half a century after Burke made the prediction, *My Trip Abroad* has yet to be rediscovered or even reissued, but it does contain a few passages of self-revelation that are worth attention, particularly Chaplin's claim that he took the trip because he needed to "get away from myself"[14]—and his dramatization of the conceit that there are at least two selves for him to escape from and that he is in danger of bouncing back and forth between them. The danger is quite literal and is described in a passage that reads like a treatment for a scene in a movie, perhaps a movie that is a further exploration of the "identity" question raised in *The Idle Class*. The occasion is the New York premiere of Douglas Fairbanks's *The Three Musketeers*. Confronting a mob, Chaplin is trapped in a terrible conundrum: if he slips into the prop smile that identifies him as Charlie, the mob will close in and tear his clothes off, but when he uses his "real" smile to open "new space in the jam," he is kept from his goal by policemen who, unable to recognize the real Chaplin, push him back to the mob he is trying to escape.

All through the book, Chaplin complains about the difficulty of escaping "himself" and his fame. He is followed everywhere on the boat and must turn to a London Bobby for protection when he finds, to no one's surprise but his own, that he cannot walk alone through the streets of his old neighborhood. "People are looking at me. . . . Who am I? For a moment I am caught unawares" (57). The last line is wonderfully ambiguous: is he caught unawares by the people on the street—or caught unawares by sudden confusion about his identity? On the train to Germany, he learns that he is practically unknown there: "This rather pleases me because I feel that I can relax and be away from crowds" (114). But once he arrives, he changes his mind: "It seems hard for me to relax and get the normal reaction to meeting people. They don't know me here. I have never been heard of. It interests me and I believe I resent it just a bit" (115).

Returning to California, Chaplin met Clare Sheridan, a tall, handsome war widow with a son the same age as Jackie Coogan. They went camping together on a wild stretch of the Pacific coast, then she and her son moved into Chaplin's mansion. Soon there were rumors and reports they would marry. To many, it seemed an ideal match: a cousin of Winston Churchill, she belonged to the British aristocracy Chaplin had delighted in meeting on his trip abroad; a sculptor, writer, and world traveler four years Chaplin's senior, she could hold her own in conversation. Beauty, breeding, intelligence, talent, and maturity were not enough, however—or were too much: Chaplin broke off the relationship.

The brief encounter with Clare Sheridan had one legacy: an independent verification of Chaplin's state of mind at that period by a good observer. "'I must get back to work,'" Chaplin told Sheridan, "'but I don't feel like it'; he was obsessed by a fear that he could no longer be funny. . . . 'I don't feel funny. Think—think of it, if I could never be funny again.'"[15]

Back at work, he repressed the urge to make another feature film and ground out *Pay Day*, a two-reeler in which Charlie is married to a nagging, larger, older woman but flirts with Edna. Full of jokes about laziness, casual theft, philandering, drunkenness, and marital wrath, the film is a final return to the old world of Sennett. *Pay Day*'s drunken ramblings, for instance, are to be found in *The Rounders*—and Phyllis Allen plays Charlie's wife in both films.

With *The Pilgrim*, released early in 1923, Chaplin continued the exploration of his screen persona. For the first time in nearly five years, he does not wear the basic costume (it will be two and a half years before we see it again). Instead, he is an escaped convict wearing stolen clerical garb. But the disguise lends no immediate sense of identity, for when a prospective bridegroom calls out to the fake parson, he runs. Taking a train West (the title is an old frontier expression for a tenderfoot or greenhorn), Pilgrim Charlie arrives in the mythical community of Devil's Gulch where he is mistaken for the new minister—and where he mistakes the sheriff's outstretched hands of welcome for a demand that he surrender. The initial mistake about the sheriff's intentions is repeated in reverse at the very end: that same sheriff gives him a chance to escape, but Charlie will be painfully slow to understand that he is free. In between those two polar scenes with the sheriff, Chaplin explores the possibilities of how Charlie reacts to a world that insists on taking him at face value as a parson. After all those early films in which Charlie borrowed costumes and identities with the intent to deceive and continue deceiving, *The Pilgrim* is different because Charlie does his best to live up to the values imposed by his borrowed identity. Thus, this final short comedy is a pilgrimage toward the two major films in which the central dramatic problem is initiated *(City Lights)* or resolved *(The Great Dictator)* by the Chaplin character accepting a new identity thrust upon him.

At the center of *The Pilgrim* is the "test" of Charlie's ability to maintain his new identity: the church service. Early on, Chaplin makes us see that the preacher-in-spite-of-himself perceives the church as a courtroom and himself the accused: when he looks toward the choir, a large "*12*" is superimposed on the image; when the Deacon (Mack Swain) brings him the hymn book, Charlie raises his hand to swear his oath like an accused felon at the bar. But a minute later, taking a sip of water, he transforms the church into another kind of bar by searching for the brass rail with his foot as he downs his drink. Finally, as Charlie pantomimes the story of David and Goliath, the church becomes a theater and the congregation both his audience and (via the camera angle) an extension of the audience in the movie theater.

The David and Goliath sermon is not in itself the sublime work of genius some critics make it out to be. It seems, rather, Chaplin's straightforward attempt to depict how an untrained mime like the convict would act out a sermon. Except for the enthusiastic response of one obnoxious child, the congregation is understandably puzzled and unmoved by the effort. Thus, when Charlie bows at the end in expectation of applause that is not forthcoming from the dour congregation, we are actually seeing Chaplin breaking through the role to bow to his larger audience.

The Pilgrim, ultimately, is an essay on role-playing and the difficulty of escaping from old roles or taking on new ones. For that reason, it ends with a battle between conflicting roles. The sheriff, having witnessed Charlie's selfless efforts on behalf of a widow and her pretty daughter (Edna Purviance, of course), does not want to take him back to prison but cannot violate his oath of office or his notion of professional responsibility by giving Charlie his freedom. "Trapped" in his role, he decides that Charlie should take it upon himself to escape and sends him off to pick flowers. But Charlie, locked into the role of prisoner once more, stubbornly refuses to recognize what is expected of him and returns with flowers. Sent across the border into Mexico to pick more flowers, Charlie stubbornly refuses to understand that there is something strange about the huge, taciturn sheriff's particularity about posies. He runs after the sheriff, who is riding away on his horse. Now the sheriff stops playing his official role and becomes one of Chaplin's first genuine human beings: he collars Charlie, drags him roughly back to the border, and kicks him across to freedom.

The film ends with Charlie's discovery that freedom is dangerous, for the territory across the border is infested with warring bandits. With prison facing him on one side of the border and life-threatening anarchy on the other, Charlie takes what narrow freedom is left: he scuttles away from the camera, one foot in the dusty American road, the other in the Mexican scrub, free only to jump in the direction of whichever danger (or freedom) seems more appealing or less appalling. For Chaplin himself, the choices would be equally difficult, for with *The Pilgrim*—a four-reeler that was accepted by First National in lieu of the last two shorter films required by the contract—he was free to do anything he wanted. But what were his limits? Where would he go now and how would he get there?

3

Master of Silence

Shadow and Substance: *A Woman of Paris*

NEWS OF THE completion of the First National contract inspired the eminent Stark Young to write an open letter to Chaplin. Eulogizing "Charlie" as one of the "great clowns of all time," Young warned that it would be physically impossible for Chaplin to sustain the role much longer. Predicting that "The spring will go out of it," Young urged Chaplin to abandon Charlie and expand his repertory with plays like *Liliom, He Who Gets Slapped,* or *Peer Gynt.* [1] By the time Young's rather inappropriate suggestions reached print in the summer of 1922, Chaplin was searching for a new part for himself. Pola Negri, with whom he was romantically linked during this period, remembers dinner companions laughing when Chaplin said he dreamed of playing Hamlet and Napoleon, a part for which he had himself costumed and photographed. [2]

Eventually, he gave up the search for a new role and made *A Woman of Paris,* a feature in which he appears for only a few seconds as a porter who drops a trunk as he walks through the frame. In *My Autobiography,* Chaplin explains that he did not play the lead in his first United Artists film because he wanted to launch Edna Purviance in a starring role that would make it possible for her to begin a career independent of him: "looking objectively at Edna, I realized she was growing rather matronly, which would not be suitable for the feminine confection necessary for my future pictures" (*A,* 296).

In addition to Chaplin's announced reason, there seems to be a more important reason why he did not play the lead opposite Edna Purviance's Marie St. Clair: there were two major male characters and each was a projection of a part of Chaplin. How could Chaplin choose between Pierre Revel, the sophisticated, cynical, wealthy, licentious man of the world, and Jean Millet, the simple artist?

Chaplin avoided having to choose by splitting his alter ego between two actors. Jean Millet is played by Carl Miller, a very weak actor who began his brief career playing romantic leads and ended it in a series of minor roles in which he was usually cast as a blackmailer, crooked stock broker, seducer, adulterer, or vengeful rejected suitor. Perhaps the main reason why Chaplin cast him in A *Woman of Paris* was that Miller had been adequate in *The Kid* as the artist who fathered the Woman's baby—that is, Chaplin felt comfortable with Miller in a variation of the kind of role played by Lloyd Bacon, whom Miller resembles. In any case, the casting of the cold-faced, unappealing Miller seems the one glaringly false note in a masterful film, for Marie's eventual regeneration must spring from her guilt over Jean's suicide. The casting of Adolphe Menjou as the playboy Pierre Revel is quite another matter. The only important actor ever employed by Chaplin until he hired Marlon Brando for his last film, Menjou was on the verge of a brilliant career when Chaplin first noticed him in a restaurant. The story goes that Chaplin's attention was called to Menjou by Peggy Hopkins Joyce, the notorious matrimonial adventurer and "gold digger" he had met while he was finishing *The Pilgrim* and looking around for the subject of his first feature for United Artists. The inspiration for the "Woman of Paris," Joyce told Chaplin that Menjou was a dead-ringer for a wealthy Parisian *bon vivant* she had been involved with.[3]

Chaplin escaped from his own involvement with Peggy Hopkins Joyce with two stories she told him: of her affair with a famous French publisher and of a young man who killed himself for her. Though these stories became the starting point for his new scenario, the speed with which he wrote the script between mid-August and November of 1922 suggests that Joyce merely triggered certain ideas that were already on his mind.[4] As we will see when we come to *The Great Dictator* and *Monsieur Verdoux*, Chaplin had the habit of giving credit to others for the ideas behind some of his most self-referential films. So with A *Woman of Paris.* Peggy Hopkins Joyce may have supplied him with a "source," but ultimately the "Woman of Paris" is Edna Purviance herself. Like the actress, the character is a girl from a small town who agrees to go to the big city with a young artist but ends up as the mistress of an entirely different man, a man whose engagement to another woman she will first learn about in the public press—and who will return to her in spite of his marital commitments. The only important difference between character and actress is that Marie St. Clair eventually breaks free of her rich lover whereas Edna Purviance would live out her life on Chaplin's payroll, a kept woman. Adolphe Menjou provides a telling piece of corroboration for the notion that A *Woman of Paris* explores the character of the actress as much as the character played by the actress: though Chaplin hired a painter to create a portrait of Edna as Marie for a scene in the film, his efforts failed to satisfy Chaplin, who then commissioned a prop man to do a life-sized crayon copy of the "cover of an old fan magazine."[5] In the film, Jean Millet sets out to do a portrait of Marie as she is, a rich man's elegant mistress, but produces a portrait based on his memory of her as a simple country girl. That memory-portrait is nothing more than a copy of an idealized representation of Edna created for the fans by Chaplin.

A *Woman of Paris* opens more slowly and statically than any other Chaplin film, before or after. First, the image of a stone house in "a small village, somewhere in France," dissolves to a closer shot of the house; then, closer still, a third shot emphasizes an upstairs window. With the fourth shot, closer to the window, we are shown Edna Purviance's face behind the sash, lit from one side, and told that she is "Marie St. Clair, a woman of fate—victim of an unhappy home." After the intertitle, Chaplin returns to the same setup as for the fourth shot, and shows us Marie biting her lip, a gesture that breaks the painterly stillness of the initial sequence of shots and provides Chaplin with the psychological opportunity to take us inside the gloomy house and the obscure life of the girl.

Once inside her bedroom, Chaplin allows Marie to throw some light on her surroundings and her actions. She lights a gas lamp, revealing two opposed artifacts of obedience and revolt: a prominently displayed crucifix on the wall and an open suitcase on the bed. Meanwhile, out in the hall, the ominous shadow of her stepfather climbs the stairs. The man himself appears and locks Marie in her room. At the window, Marie looks out again as Chaplin cuts back to the initial view from the street to introduce Jean Millet lighting a cigarette in the foreground while Marie watches from the window in the background. Opening another window, she delivers the first line of the film, "I'm locked in." And indeed she is and will continue to be—locked in by her stepfather and by "Destiny" and "Public Opinion," the concepts that gave the film its first two working titles.

Having established the oppressive conditions of the house in which Marie lives, Chaplin has Marie escape through an upstairs window so she and Jean can discuss their plans to elope to Paris in the morning. When they return to find she is locked out, Jean brings her home with him, but a second paterfamilias casts his shadow and orders Marie from the house. Then Jean's father dies, apparently of a stroke precipitated by Marie's presence in his house. After these shadowy doings, Chaplin shifts the scene to the train station, where the arrival of the Paris train is seen only as shadows cast by a cardboard cutout. Chaplin subtitles the film "A Drama of Fate," but his notion of "fate" seems to consist of murky coincidences and ominous mechanical contrivances that are mere pasteboard. Almost as though mocking himself, Chaplin will, near the end, play one more shadow trick involving a "father" figure—but this one will be a figure of light who beams approvingly on Marie.

Between the shadows of the first and the last father figures fall the adventures of Marie in Paris, the "city of light," where we discover her a year later (via the magic of ellipsis) entering a luxurious, brightly lit night club at the side of Pierre Revel, "A gentleman of leisure, whose whims have made and ruined many a woman's career." Within moments of his entrance, the elegant corruption of Pierre is made graphic and tangible through a series of shots that begins with a kitchen boy's disgusted reaction as he takes an overripe specimen of fowl from a meat locker. As this stinking foulness is carried through the kitchen at arm's length by the boy, it offends the sensibilities of at least three other flunkies, but when it reaches Pierre, it meets the standards of his refined tastes. By showing the reactions of the common clay to the rotten bird, Chaplin enlists the audience's own memories of the stench of corruption. At this point, without benefit of direct commentary by Chaplin, we have the two extremes that surround Marie: the dark village fathers who can tolerate no whiff or taint of corruption —and the glittering Pierre, who seems to revel in it.

Next comes a sexually suggestive but censor-proof morning sequence showing Marie and Pierre in bed—in different apartments. First a friend, Fifi, enters to rouse Marie; opening the windows to let in fresh air (and let out any lingering scent of the mutual corruption of Pierre and Marie), Fifi good-naturedly chides Marie for "wasting your life in bed," an oblique reference to her new occupation. Then we cut to what an intertitle identifies as the "business office of Pierre Revel": his bed chamber. Pierre is in bed, reading a stock ticker and giving orders to his secretary. Glancing at a magazine, he notices the announcement of his forthcoming marriage to the daughter of a wealthy family—"EVENT WILL LINK LARGE FORTUNE," runs the caption, indirectly suggesting another way that business is conducted in bed.

With the announcement of Pierre's impending marriage, Chaplin is ready to prepare us for the film's major conflict: Marie's choice between two ways of life. Having demonstrated in the paired village and night club scenes that the life of a fallen woman in Paris seems preferable to (or at least more interesting than) the old life she was preparing to escape with Jean, who remained behind in the village after his father's sudden death, Chaplin sets the audience up for the return of Jean to the plot in a scene between Marie and Pierre. Telling her that his marriage will make no difference to them, Pierre leaves the distraught Marie with the good manners and good sense of his kind: "I'll see you tomorrow when you are in a better mood." Chaplin fades out on the weeping Marie—and with the good sense for pacing of his kind takes us immediately to a wild party in a Latin Quarter studio.

The transition is so abrupt that at least two of Chaplin's biographers, Theodore Huff and John McCabe, have made the mistake of asserting that Pierre calls Marie from the party when in fact the call is made by one of Marie's girl friends (and Pierre is not even in evidence at the party). Following vague directions symbolic of the choices facing her ("It's the studio on the right or left, I don't know which"), Marie winds up at the studio of Jean Millet, who has come to live in Paris. Between the phone call and the reunion, however, Chaplin entertains and distracts us with a striptease involving a presumably naked woman who is unwrapped like a mummy from a winding sheet, her statuesque pose prefiguring the nude statue under which Jean will kill himself as a result of his chance reunion with Marie, the unintentional femme fatale.

Marie's arrival at the building where she must make a choice between "the studio on the right or left" returns her to the dimness and atmospheric pools of light we have not seen since she left her village. Pausing at the door to the building, she stands directly under a light that excludes the rest of the world. The hallway of the studio building is equally dark and drab, again like her village home and unlike anything we have seen elsewhere in Paris. Clearly, she has begun to return to the murky moral and luminous values represented by the village. To one side, the left, is the source of the only light. Momentarily attracted to this "sinister" light, she turns away to knock on the "right" door, the one that leads back to Jean and darkness. After cutting to inside Jean's studio to show how dimly lit and drab it is, Chaplin surprises us by having a totally unexpected light flood out of the studio, blanching Marie. The effect, like so much in this film, is largely symbolic and expressionistic—and confusing, for Jean does not represent the way of light for Marie, who must find the way on her own after his final descent into darkness.

Marie's "regeneration" begins with Jean's efforts to restore Marie to the way she was before she became "a woman of Paris." First he paints a portrait of her dressed in the nunlike outfit she wore in the village. Then he asks her to marry him. Tempted to accept the offer, she changes her mind when she overhears Jean admit to his mother that he proposed in a moment of weakness. Rejected by Marie, Jean kills himself—an act that makes no sense other than as a narrative and symbolic hook for the final "enlightenment" scene: returning from Marie's apartment where she had gone to murder the femme fatale, Jean's mother enters the dark studio to find Marie praying for forgiveness over her son's body as light floods down from above and the portrait of Marie-as-she-was hovers ghostlike in the gloomy background.

In spite of the beauty of the composition, Chaplin does not end the
scene with the "painterly" image of Marie kneeling in the center of a
frame balanced on the left by the dark figure of Jean's mother and on the
right by the dark portrait of Marie. Instead, he shows us the vengeful
mother's reaction to what she sees: she puts down her pistol as the scene
ends with a cut to the blackness that serves as a transition to the
brightness of the final scene. To understand why Chaplin did not cut
back to the beautiful composition, we need to look at the end of the scene
immediately before the one in the studio. When Jean's mother leaves
Marie's apartment, Chaplin holds the shot for several seconds so that we
see an elegant composition of light fixtures and vases at the center of
which is an eighteenth-century French painting of courtiers at play in a
pastoral setting. The extreme formality of Chaplin's arrangement of the
framed painting at the center of a foyer framed by curtains in the center
of a frame empty of humans calls attention to its own formality. But the
end of the "enlightenment" scene, with the mother moving away from
the pistol, calls attention to what will happen after the shot: the offscreen reconciliation of Marie and Jean's mother. The first composition
is closed, "locked-in", the second is open; the first suggests an end, the
second a new beginning.

The "false" pastoral icon in Marie's apartment is balanced and con-
trasted at the start of the last part of the film. An iris opens to reveal a
stone cottage—not one of the grim, crowded, nocturnal dwellings we
saw at the start, but a vine-covered rural retreat standing by itself in the
sun behind a picket fence. Now the lushly maternal qualities of Edna/
Marie are fully developed: she and Jean's mother are discovered caring
for at least four or five small children. "Mother," a child calls, "here
comes Father!" As at the start, a large male shadow comes into frame,
but it is cast by a figure in the sun, not the artificial light of the opening
scenes. And "Father" is a jovial priest who asks Junoesque Marie when
she is going to marry and have children of her own.

The film ends with Marie riding in the back of a horse-drawn cart on
her way home with fresh milk. From the opposite direction comes
Pierre's big touring car. "Whatever became of Marie St. Clair?" asks
Pierre's companion. Pierre shrugs and the old lovers pass without seeing
one another as an iris closes around the image of the cart disappearing up
the dusty road away from us. This ending is so understated that some
critics remember more than is there—Lewis Jacobs, trying to add
conflict and excitement, speaks of the cart being "forced off the road by
[Pierre's] high-powered motor car."[6] More revealing than Jacob's careless exaggeration is the dissatisfaction with the simplicity of this happy
ending (one of Marie's "children" is beside her and the farmers in the
cart are singing to the music of an accordion) that leads McCabe, Huff,

Manvell, and others to recount the spurious legend that Chaplin shot a sophisticated, cynical alternate ending (for release in Europe) in which Marie goes back to Pierre. There is no record of such an ending. Although *A Woman of Paris* was a failure at the box office (for the first time in his career, Chaplin lost money on a film) and was quickly withdrawn from circulation, it was generally well received by the critics and was a seminal influence on other filmmakers. It is a critical commonplace that the "Lubitsch touch" was refined by Ernst Lubitsch's enthusiasm for Chaplin's film. Michael Powell, a young office worker who would eventually direct such classics as *The Red Shoes, Stairway to Heaven,* and *Peeping Tom,* decided to change jobs after seeing *A Woman of Paris:* "I reckoned that if the film was capable of this sort of subtlety, it was the medium for me."[7]

And yet, Chaplin did not do anything in *A Woman of Paris* that he had not done before—he simply did it in a way that seemed different. Though he would speak of how he set out to achieve subtle emotional and psychological effects in *A Woman of Paris,* he had already done so in *The Tramp* and *The Kid,* to name two examples. *A Woman of Paris* was a serious film, but so were many of his earlier films—and this one was also very funny, particularly in Pierre Revel's cynical delight in the follies of lesser mortals. The problem was that Chaplin had allowed the world to see the Olympian side of himself—that he had, like Charlie in *The Idle Class,* opened the suit of armor hiding Chaplin. And the world had responded, "that's not Charlie, where's he gone off to?" Even as his most faithful admirers were puzzling their way through *A Woman of Paris,* Chaplin was about to put on his old costume—and Charlie was going for the gold.

Dancing on the Brink: *The Gold Rush*

On his way to New York for the premiere of *A Woman of Paris,* Chaplin told reporters in Chicago that he intended to abandon slapstick humor for a more whimsical variety. A week after the premiere, and when he knew that his old mass audience would not accept radical departures, Chaplin corrected himself so forcefully that a *New York Times* article opened with the flat assertion, "Charlie Chaplin will never renounce the slapstick."[8] In *My Autobiography,* he speaks of how he was "anxious to top the success of *The Kid*": "I kept saying to myself: 'This next film must be an epic! The greatest!' But nothing would come." Then, Chaplin tells us, one Sunday morning at Doug Fairbanks's house, he picked up a stereoscope and looked at views of gold-crazed prospectors climbing a snowy mountain in the Klondike: "Immediately ideas and comedy business began to develop, and, although I had no story, the image of one began to grow" (A, 303).

The power of that first impression stayed with Chaplin, who would eventually open the film on the image of an incredibly long line of prospectors stretched out across a snow-covered mountain slope. Working, he claims, without a script, he began shooting scenes appropriate to the Far North, including a discarded "love scene with an Eskimo girl who teaches the tramp to kiss in Eskimo fashion" (A, 304). But he quickly ran into problems. "I had an agonizing time with *The Gold Rush*, trying to motivate it," he told an interviewer many years later. "You say to yourself, what do I do? In *The Gold Rush*, you'll find gold. So what? What happens then? How damn dull are all the stories of the great North and Alaska. . . . I thought of snow. I thought of freezing and taking his socks off and they stood up, his trousers stood up. . . . But what happens after that? Then I got into a single situation: hunger. I got that from reading about the Donner party . . . starving to death, [turning to] cannibalism, eating shoe strings and everything. And I thought, 'Oh yes, there's something *funny* in that.'"[9]

With those two discoveries, Chaplin had struck a pair of seams that would lead him to a mother lode of greatness. The first seam, the Alaskan gold rush itself, is largely responsible for the epic nature and lasting fame of the movie. Singling out *The Gold Rush* and Buster Keaton's Civil War chase *The General* as the only comic epics produced during the silent era, Walter Kerr salutes Chaplin's wisdom in rooting his comedy in an "historical moment . . . so representative that it take on mythological status. . . . The Alaskan gold rush was virtually the climax, hence an ultimate symbol, of a country's discovery and mastery of its natural resources; a 'mountain of gold' was the equivalent of every immigrant's dream of 'streets paved with gold.'"[10] What made it possible for Chaplin to "get inside" the epic story was his attention to the smaller, more personal seam—hunger. Though he started with the physical hunger for food, he soon began to draw connections between the hunger for gold and for love and companionship as well. And though the specific inspiration was a group of snowbound "pilgrims" in California a few years before the gold rush of 1849, hunger was a theme that had been important to Chaplin in earlier films and would now reach such epic proportions that Charlie, literally hungry enough to eat a bear, would be driven to eating part of his own legend: to sharing his own shoe with a ravenous prospector who would then try to eat the man behind the legend.

The Gold Rush, which took nearly two years to produce, came close to consuming Chaplin himself, for in the process of making it (and in some ways because he was making it), he got married for the second time and fathered two children under circumstances that led to scandal, heartbreak, and an eventual emotional collapse. Having to find a new female lead for the first time in nearly a decade, he announced a talent search for a young actress to play the only kind of girl who would be genuinely appropriate to a story set during a gold rush: a gold-digging "dance hall" girl. Thus began what the popular press proclaimed the "second" gold rush—the second scramble for a share of Chaplin's personal fortune—for as a result of the talent search, Lillita McMurray, the flirting angel of *The Kid*, reentered his life. Though his assistants were not impressed by he fifteen-year-old's screen test, Chaplin was enchanted. Giving her a new name, Lita Grey, and star treatment, he put her under contract to play the cold-hearted vixen Charlie falls in love with. For what happened next, we must turn to Lita Grey Chaplin's autobiography: according to her uncontested account, he seduced and deflowered her, took no contraceptive precautions and told her none were necessary, got her pregnant, refused to marry her, insisted she have an abortion, called her a whore repeatedly, threatened her with violence, married her under compulsion in a melodramatic wedding trip that seemed "the peculiar inspiration of someone deranged,"[11] ignored her after the marriage, bribed her doctor to postdate the baby's birth certificate so the birth would seem to come a merely premature seven months after the marriage rather than five, and got her pregnant again—all before *The Gold Rush* was finished.

None of this scandal and pain really matters, except to increase our appreciation of the conditions under which Chaplin managed to create a remarkably gentle and forgiving film about isolation, humiliation, and suffering. Ultimately, the many delays brought on by the crises in his personal life may have contributed to the brilliance of the film by slowing him down and giving him reasons to redo many parts that did not please him totally. After shooting miles of footage with Lita Grey over a period of eight or nine months, he removed her from the picture and re-created her scenes with Georgia Hale. After so many false starts, the result was a narrative that approached perfection. His personal life might be confused and marred by mistakes and errors in judgment, but with his film he could go back and do it right: "What I have done in *The Gold Rush*," he told a reporter, "is exactly what I want to do. I have no excuses, no alibis. I have done just as I liked with this picture."[12]

When we consider these setbacks and disasters, the final achievement becomes as remarkable as that of Charlie and his partner surviving cold, hunger, amnesia, and the wildly tilting cabin to discover the mountain of gold. In *My Autobiography* (305) and *My Life in Pictures* (227), Chaplin describes the emotional and economic payoff of *The Gold Rush* in exactly the same words: the United Artists sales manager came up and "embraced me [saying] 'Charlie, I guarantee that it will gross at least six million dollars'—and it did!" The embrace of the sales manager—and of the loving, understanding, forgiving public is foreshadowed and invited in the film's two emotional climaxes: first Charlie's partner embraces him with the news that they have discovered the mountain of gold, then Charlie and the dance hall girl embrace to end the movie.

The Gold Rush is basically circular in structure, opening with many struggling prospectors trekking into the Klondike, ending with two successful survivors voyaging home in luxury. In between, there are two major life-and-death struggles (the first against hunger, the second against gravity) in a lonely cabin; in turn, these scenes bracket the structural and emotional center of the film, the scenes set in the dance hall where Charlie meets the girl and in the second cabin where he plays host to her. In essence, the film has a five-act structure, with very short first and fifth acts (the journey in and the journey out), longer second and fourth acts (Charlie and his partner in the lonely cabin), and a very long middle act that ends with a double climax: Charlie gets a love note intended for someone else and is immediately promised a fortune if he can lead his partner back to the lonely cabin.

Filmed in the mountains of northern California within a few miles of the area where the Donner Party was stranded by snow, the first sequence looks almost documentary. Chaplin opens on a series of epic images: hundreds of prospectors strung out across the snow, the individuals in the foreground merging to form a continuous black line against the whiteness. As we get closer through editing, we see one prospector collapse from exhaustion in the foreground. He remains motionless for a long beat while others tramp past him. Then, with another epic long shot, Chaplin reestablishes the base camp, the snowy expanse, and the steep mountains, all connected by an endless single file of men. Irising out, Chaplin supplies an intertitle: "Three days from anywhere. A lone Prospector." Now Charlie appears in the costume we have not seen since *Pay Day* over three years before—and which Chaplin will wear in one form or another for the next fifteen years. Never before had it been so totally inappropriate to his environment.

With the appearance of Charlie, the film shifts suddenly (and for the most part permanently) to a studio set of plaster cliffs and salt snow. A tiny black figure in the heart of whiteness, he does his trademark skidding turn around the corner of an icy ledge as though it is a city sidewalk and is joined by a very large black bear. The bear, unnoticed by Charlie, enters a cave and Chaplin cuts to Big Jim McKay (Mack Swain), a fur-clad figure who looks and sometimes acts suspiciously like a bear—and who will later seem (in Charlie's misapprehension) to be transformed into one by ravenous hunger. Noteworthy here is that immediately after noticing Charlie frolicking in the snow, Big Jim discovers his mountain of gold, a strike he will not be able to recover without the help of the talismanic Charlie.

Back to Charlie looking at a map. Which way will he (and the narrative) go? But the map is surrealistically basic: a cross with the compass points but no land features. Following his "map," he finds an equally surrealistic marker for the grave of a prospector who got lost in the snow on "Friday 1898." Lost in time and space, Charlie scurries on until a storm blows him into the lonely cabin of a desperado named Black Larsen (played by Tom Murray, the threatening but sympathetic sheriff in *The Pilgrim*). Black Larsen orders him to leave, and Charlie tries, but the storm keeps blowing him back in. There is something that wants Charlie in that cabin, some force that knows Charlie cannot be led there by a man-made map or ordered thence by a mere human. That force is Chaplin, the storm his brainstorm, the wind his inspiration, for Chaplin knows he must get his characters inside the cabin in order to tell a meaningful human story and to fight against the narrative entropy of the studio landscape.

Once the wind blows Big Jim McKay into the cabin, Chaplin is ready for his first major dramatic and thematic confrontations. Charlie sneaks up to see whether the huge, bear-skinned creature is man or beast, a matter left unresolved when Big Jim snatches the bone Charlie was gnawing on and nearly eats Charlie's hand in the process. Recovering his hand, Charlie strokes Big Jim's fur, making a "nice doggy" gesture and beginning the slow development of the partnership that leads to the sharing of the mountain of gold—and parallels the stages of Charlie's late friendship with the dance hall girl.

The partnership between Charlie and Big Jim is first tested, then cemented through food. After Charlie gobbles down the last edible in the cabin (a candle stub), the three starving men cut cards to see who will go in search of food. Black Larsen loses the cut and quickly happens upon and kills two bounty-hunters. As Black Larsen hauls away their sled with all its provisions, Chaplin inserts an intertitle, "Thanksgiving Dinner," that seems to suggest that the hungry trio will share Black Larsen's plunder; it refers, instead, to the eating of Charlie's boiled shoe, a marvellously conceived gag that paves the way for the cannibalism gag to come. Immediately after the shoe-fest, we see Black Larsen, "Indifferent to his comrades' plight," as he stumbles on Big Jim's mountain of gold. Back in the cabin, Charlie returns empty-handed from hunting. He offers to cook the other shoe, but Big Jim cannot stomach that idea. Suddenly, Charlie turns into a chicken, then back into a man, and again into a chicken. When Big Jim tries to shoot Charlie-the-Chicken, the man reappears. Thinking about what he has almost done, Big Jim decides it does not really make any difference: "Chicken or no chicken, his friend looks appetizing." With Charlie in danger of following his shoe down Big Jim's gullet, a cut to Black Larsen frying some stolen meat beside Big Jim's claim reinforces the point: in this world, claims are to be jumped, comrades abandoned or eaten—unless fate or nature intervene. The intervention begins when Big Jim wakes up hungry and attacks Charlie until a bear ambles in and scares him off. Just as Big Jim hallucinated that Charlie had turned into a chicken, Charlie thinks Big Jim has literally become a ravening beast. Recovering from his shock, he shoots the bear, orders Big Jim to fetch it, and begins setting the table for dinner.

With the satisfaction of the need for shelter and food, Chaplin is ready for the romantic interest at the heart of the film. But first, he has Big Jim go to his mountain of gold, where he is attacked by Black Larsen and left to die moments before a snowy ledge gives way under the villain and plunges him to his death in retaliation for his crimes against good fellowship.

Cutting to a nameless boom town, Chaplin introduces us to Georgia as she enters a photo studio to pick up the portrait she has commissioned. Remarkably, no one seems to have paid attention to the graphic fact that Georgia is, when first and last seen, directly or indirectly the object of a camera. Only after he introduces Georgia and "Jack, the Ladies Man" (a prosperous dance hall patron with a mustache similar to Pierre Revel's), does Chaplin bring Charlie back into the story. Having sold his pick and shovel, given up his gold-digging, Charlie enters the Monte Carlo dance hall (an interesting name, containing a reference to Charlie's name as well as to the famous casino where fortunes are easily won and lost) and sees Georgia just after she tears one of her photographs trying to get it back from Jack. Representative of the divided self of the girl who is attracted to and repelled by Jack and all he represents, the torn photograph, like the girl, will be put back together by Charlie. But before she can be restored to wholeness by her relationship to Charlie, Chaplin must motivate Charlie's attraction to the girl—and hers to him.

The first part of the process is simple: lonely Charlie, hearing his name and seeing the smiling girl walk toward him with her hand held out in welcome, and not knowing she is heading for another, handsomer "Charlie" behind him, is stricken with romantic optimism. Frozen out by the girl's indifference to him, Charlie fights back by taking someone else's dose of liquid warmth from a passing tray of whiskey. A minute or so after capturing Charlie's eye, Georgia confides to a friend that she is bored: "If I could only meet someone worthwhile—I'm so tired of this place." Charlie overhears this, of course, and both he and the audience wait breathlessly as she begins to scan the room for such a man—and looks right at Charlie without seeing him. A minute later, refusing to dance with Jack, she looks around to find someone so despicable, so pathetic, that by dancing with him she can show Jack how little she thinks of him, how much better she can do. Of course, she chooses the startled Charlie, and of course Charlie has no idea he is simply a pawn in someone else's game.

With the invitation to the dance comes the first step in Georgia's pas de deux with Charlie. She will laugh at him when he gets dragged off the floor by a huge dog, but at least she laughs. Her boredom relieved for a moment, she gives Charlie a soiled rose, token of her soiled self. Instantly, Charlie becomes Georgia's guardian, reluctantly fighting and accidentally defeating Jack to "protect" her from his not-unwanted attentions. Thinking himself a hero, Charlie swaggers out of the Monte Carlo with the same panache we see at the end as he saunters into view as a multimillionaire.

At this point, the exact middle of the film, Chaplin reprises the first cabin scenes by reducing the struggle for shelter and food to a picaresque trick: Charlie pretends to be frozen outside the cabin of Hank Curtis (played by Henry Bergman, who is constantly associated with food in Chaplin's films—partly because Bergman owned a popular restaurant). Curtis carries him in, feeds him, and loans him the cabin when he goes prospecting. Snug-built of logs and with but a single door against entropy, Curtis's cabin stands in direct contrast to Black Larsen's drafty plank shack with its triple entrance. Three doors and more playing space were necessary in the cabin of larceny for all the comings and goings—but only one important entrance, Georgia's, will be made to the cabin of courtesy.

Charlie invites Georgia and three other girls from the dance hall into the warm, cozy cabin and runs around outside to gather firewood and release his emotions. Meanwhile, Georgia, sitting on Charlie's humble bed, discovers she is already "in" his bed in the form of the torn photograph and wilted rose under his pillow. She shares this secret with her bawdy friends and warns them to stop laughing so she can vamp Charlie when he returns. In *My Autobiography*, Chaplin explains the narrative function of this cruel escalation of her earlier deception of Charlie: "logically it was difficult to get a beautiful girl interested in a tramp. . . . In *The Gold Rush* the girl's interest in the tramp started by her playing a joke on him, which later moves her to pity" (A, 210).

When Charlie comes inside, he joins Georgia on the bed. In a last return to the sexual naughtiness of his earlier films, Chaplin has Charlie suddenly feel the need to cross his legs so that one highly flammable portion of his anatomy (the rag-wrapped foot on which he has accidentally poured kerosene while filling a lantern) ends up under the seat of a fat girl (who has carelessly dropped a burning match onto the rags).

Hunger literally consumed Charlie's shoe; now passion for Georgia symbolically and literally threatens to consume him even further. A delightful visualization of the platitude, "people who play with fire get burned," the "fire gag" is an objective correlative for what will happen to Georgia: although it is the fat girl who gets burned by the effort to make sport of Charlie, Georgia will eventually be burned more deeply by her own sense of shame for having toyed with Charlie's feelings. "I guess you're lonesome here?" she asks, winking at her friends. "Why don't you invite us to dinner sometimes?" Suspecting that the girls are used to trifling with men, Charlie asks if they will really come to dinner. Not understanding that this is a world in which men will kill for food—or perhaps understanding it all too well—Georgia and her friends set a date they have no intention of keeping, for it is a busy night in a trade that profits on loneliness: New Year's Eve.

And so we come to the dinner scene. That heavily laden table—which Charlie has set by hiring himself out to shovel the common enemy, snow—is, in the words of Stanley Kauffmann, a "mirror image of the hunger theme" having an effect like that of Dickens's great feasts where "plentiful food does not mean gluttony, but love: an atmosphere of community, conviviality, and affection."[13] There is community, conviviality, and affection at the Monte Carlo, but it seems forced, desperate, and reeks of alienation; it is like the lonely "feast" of Black Larsen, for it leads to moral death, to the sadness of old men dancing with one another. Chaplin cuts back and forth a dozen times between the under-cranked, noisy (yes, even in a silent film) chaos of the dance hall and the quiet, dignified formality of the cabin, building to the contrast of the public reality and the private dream.

The dream: waiting for his guests, Charlie sighs and dissolves into the fantasy that he is a tremendous success as a host. He presumes to entertain dancers by "dancing" for them above the "footlights" of the dinner candles. Whereas at Thanksgiving, his shoe became food, now dinner rolls become little shoes connected to Charlie's head without the inconvenience of an intervening body. When the girls applaud, Chaplin dissolves the scene to reveal that Charlie is asleep—and fades out.

The reality: after the midnight revelry at the dance hall awakens Charlie, Chaplin contrasts close-ups of lonely Charlie in the cabin and equally lonely, remorseful dance hall girls alone with their thoughts as they share in singing Auld Lang Syne. Emphasizing one sad, hard-looking woman whose lost girlhood is well behind her, and whose face and mood "predicts" what is ahead for Georgia (the same actress would play the Gypsy fortune teller who tells the heroine of Chaplin's next film what is in store for her), Chaplin sets us up for the matched resolutions that will allow the three central characters to leave the frozen north: the recovery of the lost mountain of gold and of Georgia's ability to feel.

Georgia's journey home begins in the midst of sudden gaiety after the sadness of Auld Lang Syne: about to share in the meager snacks being passed around, she abruptly remembers her dinner date. Still callous and shameless, she proposes to Jack (her earlier aloofness was apparently only a gambit) that they go to the cabin to tease Charlie. On the way, she asks Jack if he loves her and rewards his answer with a kiss. Meanwhile, Charlie approaches the dance hall, looks through the window, and drifts away into darkness. His loneliness outside the place he does not feel he can enter is almost immediately paralleled by Georgia's sadness when she enters the warm cabin by herself and discovers how much loving care he has put into preparing for his unworthy guests. Jack comes in to demand another kiss, but Georgia pushes him away: in this place of the heart, she is no longer under the influence of the bawdy, tawdry, fickle surroundings of the dance hall. "The joke has gone too far," she tells the other girls. Not understanding her mood, or not caring, Jack tries to steal a kiss and is again rebuffed. When he forces a kiss, she slaps him and flees the cabin. The scene ends with Jack slamming the door. Before fading out, Chaplin holds on the door for a long punctuational beat to tell us we will never return there: the cabin of "courtesy" has served its purpose.

With that fade out, Chaplin is ready for the sequence of events leading up to the return to the first cabin. He opens on Big Jim McKay wandering into town, no more able to find his gold mine than Georgia can find the place where her own inner wealth is hidden. That both need Charlie is reinforced by the similarity between the way Georgia fruitlessly panned the dance hall for someone worthwhile and looked right through Charlie and the way Big Jim now looks around for Charlie but cannot see him though they are standing back to back. Will Big Jim ever notice Charlie and recover his mountain of gold? Will Georgia rediscover him in a way that will allow her to recover the heart of gold all movie whores are supposed to possess?

For both, the situation looks bleak. Big Jim wanders away from Charlie and in the dance hall that night we see a repentant Georgia writing a note without a salutation: "I'm sorry for what I did last night. Please forgive me. I love you. Georgia." Like Big Jim, she has her own brand of amnesia and has already forgotten Charlie. She sends the note to Jack who sneers at it and passes it on to Charlie, who cares only for the message and knows nothing of the medium by which it has reached him. This practical joke by Jack wipes out the ones by Georgia, who becomes as much a victim as Charlie. In terms appropriate to the claim-jumping of Black Larsen and to Big Jim's inability to register his strike because he does not know where his claim is located, Jack has conveyed the record of his claim on Georgia to Charlie.

In search of Georgia, Charlie runs around the dance hall so frantically that Big Jim finally spots him. The two men begin a shouting match, identifying their separate but linked goals: "THE CABIN!"; "GEORGIA!"; "THE CABIN!"; "GEORGIA!" Going back with Big Jim to find that mountain of gold means making money, but it also means playing house again, and Chaplin associates playing house with love. Cooking that shoe for Big Jim, setting the table after sending out the man of the house to fetch in the bear—in our memories these things can be recalled with the same fondness as the details of the early, struggling days of a marriage. And let us not forget that in Keystone's *A Busy Day,* Chaplin played Swain's shrewish wife. *The Gold Rush* will end with Charlie announcing his impending marriage to Georgia, but that marriage is prefigured in the housekeeping and symbolic marriage of Charlie and Big Jim.

Well-provisioned now with meat and flour, Charlie and Big Jim settle into their old "home." During the night, a storm blows the cabin to the mountain of gold (a reversal of the force that blew Big Jim from his claim to the cabin). They awake in "blissful ignorance" and do that strange dance on the brink of disaster in the tilting cabin scene that parallels the ups and downs, the disequilibrium of the love story. And just as Georgia temporarily forgets Charlie, Big Jim momentarily does the same when he climbs out of the doomed cabin to discover it has brought him back to his gold. But he does remember in time (or, touchingly, the cabin waits patiently until he remembers, held only by a piece of rope caught on an outcropping of the mountain of gold) and Charlie ends up in his arms. The embrace of Big Jim—so awful at first, so wonderfully protective and celebratory at last— is even more powerful than the later embrace of Charlie and Georgia on which the film ends.

"Homeward bound on the good ship success," portly Big Jim (as elegant as Edward VII, the monarch of Chaplin's youth) and top-hatted, fur-coated Charlie (as blasé and natty as the millionaire in *The Idle Class*) are sharing another "cabin"—an elegant stateroom. All that comes between their perfect union is the expensively framed but still-torn photograph of Georgia on the table between their two beds. And all that remains for Chaplin is to find a way to bring Georgia back into the story in order to join the two halves of this motion picture. The search for a narrative bond to join the two halves, love and money, must have been particularly interesting to the millionaire Chaplin who had already made two bad marriages to women he suspected were attracted to his fortune and name. Even if he could not get it right for himself, he had to find the right solution for Charlie, a solution that would test the truth of Georgia's feelings.

Bedeviled and hounded by the press in real life, Chaplin hit upon the self-referential gimmick that a reporter would ask Charlie (as many asked Chaplin) to take off his luxurious new clothes in order to be photographed for the masses in the old tramp costume in which he made his fortune. This gimmick is not simply a mechanical plot device, however—it is part of the constant process of restoration in the film: the gold is restored to Big Jim, Georgia to herself, and now, after the new costume documents his success, the famous old costume restores the girl to Charlie and Charlie to the girl as well as to the audience.

Here is how it works: when the elegantly dressed Charlie retires to the "cabin" to change, he sadly contemplates the photograph of the "lost" Georgia as his valet closes the black curtains to give him privacy. Chaplin uses the blackness to set up a cut to Georgia as she watches the crew searching for a stowaway. She is down on the cold open deck in steerage; why she has decided to leave the Klondike is not explained, which leaves us free to assume Charlie had something to do with her change of mind or heart. Cutting back to the cabin for the theatrical parting of the black curtains and the reappearance of the old Charlie with one foot wrapped in rags, the magician prepares to work his final trick. It begins with a disappearing act: obeying the photographer, Charlie steps back and drops out of frame, falling for Georgia or at least down to her level. Naturally, she thinks this ragged figure is the stowaway and forces him to hide. Caught in her act by a ship's officer, she offers to pay Charlie's fare. Look closely as Georgia begs for mercy toward the tattered tramp: that may seem to be Charlie in the costume, but the smile is the confident public smile we see in photographs and newsreel clips of Chaplin himself. For just an instant, it is Chaplin the director standing there, watching and approving the artifice of the young actress as she projects sincerity.

Some contemporary reviewers and a few later critics were unhappy about the happy ending—but Chaplin had already anticipated them in the form of the reporter who is surprised by the final kiss: "Oh! You've spoilt the picture." Quite the contrary: Charlie has replaced the torn picture of the divided Georgia with a complete one that includes himself. In doing so, Chaplin joined the two parts of his own picture.

Fear of Falling: *The Circus*

With *The Gold Rush*, Chaplin had ascended his own mountain of gold. The public loved it and the critics called it his best work. But having climbed the highest peak of his own career (and, some would say, of film art itself), what could Chaplin do next? How could he ever be as funny again? Would he even try to make another comedy right away? He considered various serious roles, including (again!) Napoleon and a virile Christ.[14] Instead, he made *The Circus*, a movie in which he risked crucifixion on the Golgotha of his most self-referential narrative premise: he would explore the nature of his own art by having Charlie become a circus performer who is funny when he does not mean to be—and who fails to amuse when he tries to get laughs. It was a daring attempt, and a dangerous one—for how could Chaplin be funny about not being funny?

A quarter century later, Chaplin would attempt a similar premise in *Limelight*, the story of an old clown who dies in his effort to recapture past glory. Published rumors about Chaplin's intentions indicate that even as *The Gold Rush* was being released, Chaplin had begun the line of thought that would lead to *Limelight*. The author of a scholarly book on comedy published in 1925 reported that Chaplin "threatens to develop the theme of a clown's unrequited love in a serious cinema tragedy."[15] That same year, Mordaunt Hall reported that Chaplin was preparing to make "a great picture on which he has set his heart" and in which he would be "clad as a circus clown except for his big shoes, his little cane and his tiny bowler hat." Entitled "The Clown," this film would "have a tragic ending—the funmaker impersonated by Chaplin is supposed to die on the tanbark while the spectators are applauding his comic pantomime."[16] Chaplin himself explains that he was planning a film about "a clown who, through an accident at the circus, has lost his sight" and who inadvertently amuses his sickly daughter by stumbling and bumping into things (A, 325).

In late 1925, when Chaplin assembled a circus complete with big top, wagons, animals, and trainers, he may have still had that tragic vision of the great picture on which he had set his heart, but by the time the film was released in early 1928, it was something entirely different. Instead of finding pathos in the sickly daughter of a blind clown, Chaplin had found it in the hungry stepdaughter of a keen-eyed ringmaster. Instead of a clown with traces of Charlie, there was Charlie in his old costume. Abandoning the notion of calling this film "The Clown," he settled on *The Circus*. The change in title is crucial, for it diffuses the emphasis on a single clown by calling attention to the entire organization. How are we to account for the difference between what Chaplin originally intended and what he accomplished? An admiring biography of Chaplin published in 1931 advances the pleasant fiction that a fire broke out during the filming of *The Circus* and "destroyed all the properties, scenes, and film and the work had to be done all over again."[17] A mere fire would have been less disastrous than what actually happened: Chaplin had come very close to burning out.

At the time of the premiere of *The Gold Rush* in New York, Chaplin seems to have collapsed physically and emotionally. With barely a month or two to recover, he plunged into what became *The Circus*. It was not a propitious time. Lita was pregnant again and the marriage was breaking up; his mother, kept remote in a cottage in the San Fernando Valley and rarely visited because her ruined mind depressed him and made it hard to work, was in poor health; Edna Purviance's attempt at an independent career had failed, partly because of her alcoholism, largely because she had no screen value other than as a blank romantic foil for Chaplin, who had plucked her out of obscurity. Before *The Circus* was finished more than two years later, he created a new film story for Edna and hired Josef von Sternberg to direct it—and then burned the result; the government sued him for back taxes in excess of a million dollars; and Lita sued for divorce.

Of all the ills that befell him during the production of *The Circus*, the worst was the divorce proceeding. Not only did Lita and her lawyers charge him with cruelty, adultery, and sexual preferences that were "abnormal, unnatural, perverted, degenerate, and indecent" (which meant nothing more than that he had expressed interest in oral sex),[18] but they also attached his holdings, which meant his home, studio, and bank accounts were closed to him, his company went unpaid, and, only a month or so short of finishing *The Circus*, he had to shut down the tremendously expensive production.

Fleeing to New York in January 1927, Chaplin seems to have had a serious nervous breakdown. His salt-and-pepper hair turned white during this period and he came to associate *The Circus* with personal and professional misery. He mentions the film only once in the text of *My Autobiography,* and then only as a digression to document the death of his mother as something that happened during the making of *The Circus* (in reality, she died during the production of *City Lights*). And when he put together *My Life in Pictures,* he devoted less space to this film than to any other of his major feature comedies—and chose to emphasize, via half a dozen stills, variations on a single image: Charlie with a gang of monkeys on his back. And yet, in spite of the chaotic events surrounding the making of *The Circus*, the film itself is calm and formal, as befits the work of a mature artist reflecting on the nature of his work, on the painful grind (common to circuses and movie studios) of producing thrills, romance, and laughter.

Perhaps because of the "trivial" setting and the easy viewing that comes from hard moviemaking, *The Circus* seems slight enough to be dismissed, as Roger Manvell does, as "a film of episodes . . . strung together along the general story line."[19] There is, however, only one clearly identifiable "episode," the scene in the lion's cage—and even that one was carefully fitted into the mosaic, as Chaplin explained to a visitor on the set: "In this film we have a continuous working story and this scene with the cage is the only bit that can really be called a gag. In other words, we are interrupting the story momentarily to put this scene in. Hence, it must be exactly right, otherwise we shall spoil the general sense and upset the audience. You are only entitled to switch from the main theme if the switching is worth while."[20] Far from "switching" away from the main theme, the scene in the lion's cage is a perfect summary of the dangers and restrictions facing Charlie, who runs into the lion's cage to escape one nemesis (a malevolent mule) just as he earlier ran into the circus to escape another (a policeman). Thus, the lion's cage is a model of the larger "trap" Charlie finds himself in: at first he is reluctant to stay in the cage (just as he had no intention to stay with the circus); then he thinks he has nothing to fear from the lion (just as he will soon stand up to the overbearing ringmaster) and dawdles in the cage to impress the girl (who is the reason why he stays with the circus as long as he does); finally he recognizes the danger and flees (just as he later survives the high wire act and forsakes the circus).

The tight organization of The Circus is encompassed by the opening and closing images. At the start, we see a paper star covering the hoop through which Merna, the bareback rider, must jump to start the movie; at the very end, Charlie, alone in the middle of a deserted circus ring, notices a torn paper star and discards it with a kick before he waddles off to his next adventure. The rupturing of the paper star by Merna in the first shot introduces us to the subject of that shot and the next two. Though it may seem logical that the first shots would focus on Merna or the clowns, the actual subject is Merna's cruel stepfather, the circus ringmaster who is an alter ego for Chaplin, the slave-driver and task-master who was the actual proprietor and ringmaster of the circus behind The Circus. It should be noted that Allan Garcia, who plays the ringmaster, also plays two other "proprietary" Chaplin alter egos: the glacial butler in City Lights and the Olympian capitalist in Modern Times. The ringmaster's distinctive costume (top hat and boots, long coat, wing collar and cravat, baggy-hipped riding breeches, and whip) looks forward to the comic animal trainer outfit Calvero wears in Limelight when he puts a lady flea through her paces—and to the riding breeches and boots affected by the Great Dictator.

By focusing the audience's attention on the ringmaster, then, Chaplin is covertly focusing on himself and his own problems as the often tyrannical proprietor of a studio that was frequently referred to as a circus. Anyone who doubts that Chaplin was a tyrant on the set should consult the accounts of how he made a frustrated elderly actress do fifty takes of a shot in *A Woman of Paris* or forced a disgusted Mack Swain to gag down shoes made of licorice for multiple takes of the "Thanksgiving Dinner" scene in *The Gold Rush*. When the ringmaster delivers the first line in the film, "You missed the hoop again," he is echoing the perfectionist Chaplin—and when he sneers at his clowns and blames them for the poor "box-office" ("Look at that house: empty!"), he is probably venting some of Chaplin's complaints. Thus, when he cast his own chief clown, Henry Bergman, as the most prominent of the dispirited, lackluster circus clowns, Chaplin was commenting on his own repertory company, a collection of mediocre performers who, like Bergman and Edna Purviance, had no appeal or careers apart from Chaplin—who had discovered, on the basis of audience reaction to *A Woman of Paris*, that he had no career apart from Charlie.

So too with the sad clowns and the weeping Merna as the first scene fades out: they need Charlie to make the circus ring with laughter and to protect the girl, who is starved and beaten by the ringmaster. When the new scene fades in, we see Charlie in an amusement park near the circus. Discovering that a pickpocket has hidden valuables on him, he tries to buy food. Immediately, the real owner of the valuables mistakes him for the thief. With brilliant efficiency, Chaplin thus introduces several of the film's central thematic concerns: that Charlie possesses hidden and unsuspected resources or talents, that he will get into trouble whenever he tries to draw on those resources, and that he will be mistaken for something or someone he is not. The similarity to the opening of *The Kid* is striking: in each film Chaplin establishes a melodramatic situation (the abandoned baby and the weeping mother; the joyless circus and the weeping girl), then drops the emotional burden on Charlie.

Escaping from the police, Charlie first runs into a hall of mirrors where the real pickpocket, the cop, Charlie, and the audience all have trouble distinguishing between the reality and the reflection; then he hides among mechanical figures by imitating them; finally, Charlie runs into the circus, where he and the pursuing cop are mistaken for clowns and where he changes places with a pretty girl in a magic act. Hired as a clown, Charlie fails to amuse—but is a hit when he stumbles around trying to be a property man. No wonder Chaplin seems to have had a nervous breakdown in the course of making this film—it is a schizoid, shifty maze of literal and figurative mirrors.

Take, for instance, the literal use of a mirror at the point Charlie becomes aware of how successful his unintentional "act" is. Overhearing a fortune teller predict that Merna will love and marry a dark, handsome man, Charlie looks into a mirror to check his image against the prediction and, delighted by what he sees, immediately plans to marry her.

Merna, meanwhile, sees and immediately falls in love with Rex, "King of the Air," a handsome young high wire artist. Jealous of Rex, Charlie begins to lose his appeal as a clown. Called upon to put on Rex's costume and replace him on the high wire, Charlie is such a poor "copy" that he is fired. Eventually Charlie sees that there are some limits to his ability to take on new roles and arranges for Merna to marry Rex. Or perhaps it is because Chaplin sees and uses the character of Rex as an extension of himself, another alter ego. The latter hypothesis becomes more attractive when we consider that Harry Crocker, who plays Rex, was Chaplin's personal friend and confidant, coauthor of the scenario, co-director of the film, and his stand-in as Charlie when Chaplin wanted to watch rehearsals from behind the camera. When Rex marries Merna, Charlie supplies the ring and "gives away" the bride, thus standing in for her stepfather, the ringmaster (when the time came for Chaplin to make his last and best marriage, he called upon Harry Crocker to return the favor by serving as his best man).

Just as Charlie is only a pale copy of Rex, *The Circus* is a pale reflection of *The Gold Rush*. Standing with his back to us, peeking through the tent to watch Merna, Charlie looks like a little boy in a Norman Rockwell painting. Compare that to the far more powerful image of the lonely figure who stands in the deathly cold darkness outside the dance hall. Charlie's fear of falling from the high wire is trivial compared to the terror of falling from (or with) the cabin into the abyss; the exploitation of the bare-back rider by her stepfather is fairy-tale stuff next to the dangers confronting Georgia, who presumably performs bare, on her back; Merna's discomfort at being sent to bed without her supper lacks the substance of the starvation facing the men in the cabin—and there is far less humor and horror in Charlie's fear that he will be eaten by a lion than in his fear he will be devoured by Big Jim. In *The Gold Rush*, Charlie physically battles and defeats Jack to establish his claim to Georgia; in *The Circus*, a pale, daydream copy of Charlie rises out of himself to knock Rex down while Charlie sits passively to one side, wishing it were so.

Even if *The Circus* is not the great film on which Chaplin claimed to have set his heart, it is far greater than most Chaplin critics concede— greater, certainly, than the faint praise Walter Kerr offers: "*The Circus* is not a poor film, it is simply the workaday product of a comic genius at odds with himself."[21] Comic geniuses at odds with themselves do not create workaday products; rather, they create flawed masterpieces that we can sometimes cherish as much as the flawless ones. And there are many reasons for cherishing *The Circus:* for its continuing ability to draw laughter, for the sheer ambition that led Chaplin to tell us what it means to be a clown, and for the fact that it is Chaplin's last silent film.

4

The Transition to Sound

City Lights and the Gift of Sight

A SUCCESS at the box office, *The Circus* earned the respect of the film industry, garnering Chaplin a special Academy Award for his "versatility and genius" as writer, star, director, and producer of a single film. There was only one other special award that year, the first year Oscars were given out: to Warner Brothers for revolutionizing the film industry by producing *The Jazz Singer* and bringing to an end the so-called "silent" era.

So much has been written about Chaplin's stubborn resistance to sound, much of it by Chaplin himself, that Gerald Mast's commentary stands out for its common sense: "The unobtrusive cinematic style of the talking films was perfectly suited to Chaplin, whose cinema style had always been unobtrusive, emphasizing what he was shooting rather than the way he was shooting it. Despite his hesitation in adopting dialogue, Chaplin's personal film style was completely consistent with the visual conventions of the dialogue film."[1]

Frequently forgotten today is the fact that most "silent" films were meant to be accompanied by elaborately orchestrated music and sound effects in the large first-run theaters. Chaplin's "silent" films were full of funny sounds, even if the sounds existed only in the minds of the audience: Eric Campbell's loud soup-slurping in *The Count*, the rattling of the alarm clock in *The Pawnshop*, the German band that drowns out Charlie's violin in *The Vagabond*, Pierre Revel's saxophone-playing while the Woman of Paris emotes, and the creaking of the cabin as it tilts in *The Gold Rush*. Looking forward to the coming of sound, one important critic had singled out Chaplin as someone who would benefit from the new technology: "I can imagine what an enormous asset a special score for *The Gold Rush* would be. Chaplin tears his hair when he hears of [the] wrong accompaniment being given his pictures, and he turns in

Chaplin with Virginia Cherrill and a silent phonograph in City Lights.

despair to mechanical devices to give him the accompaniment he wants."[2]

The great irony of his transition to sound is that Chaplin set out to mock the "talkies" and ended up with a synchronized sound picture which reminds us of how a properly orchestrated "silent" picture would have sounded before 1927. With close to a hundred distinct musical cues and a powerful set of motifs associated with major characters and abstractions (love, hope, defeat), *City Lights* bridges the two major eras of film history. And yet, in *My Autobiography* Chaplin referred to *City Lights* and its even "noisier" successor, *Modern Times*, as "silent" (A, 366, 383). Late in life, he told an interviewer that he shot *City Lights* as a silent film and was forced by United Artists to add an unwanted sound track.[3] Though this claim seems false in the light of the complex use of visual clues for sound in *City Lights*, it is typical of the statements that resulted in Chaplin being considered the lone holdout against sound. Perhaps he announced that he would sell his old studio and build a new one where others could join him in producing nothing but silent films[4] for the same reason that he constantly asserted his desire to play Hamlet, Christ, or Napoleon: an attention-getting mixture of stubbornness, megalomania, wishful thinking, and a playful desire to shock, amuse, and tease his public. In retrospect, Chaplin's fabled resistance to sound appears to have been a game in which he talked endlessly about why he would not speak in movies while going about the business of making genuine sound films that tell us far more about the possibilities of film sound than most of the competition.

For decades, Chaplin's critics have "explained" Chaplin's alleged silence. Typically, some have reported that Chaplin was reluctant to switch to sound because he would no longer be able to undercrank scenes for comic effect because the early sound cameras had to be operated at a constant twenty-four frames per second.[5] That explanation is blown away when we notice that some of the earliest sound films, including *The Jazz Singer* and Chaplin's own *City Lights* and *Modern Times*, have undercranked scenes that retain the fast movement of the silent screen. Although it is sometimes asserted that Charlie never spoke, he did indeed and with a "voice" that ranged from barely articulate ("I'm so h-h-happy," he stutters in *The Gold Rush*) to forceful rhetoric (look again at the scene in which he persuades Rex to marry Merna in *The Circus*), from shy whispers to bold shouts (as for Georgia's attention in *The Gold Rush*). There was no reason for Chaplin to fear the coming of sound or its use. A clever mimic with a voice that recorded well, he had used mood music effectively in making his silent films and would later take pride in composing most of the music for his sound films and for the sound versions of the films he made before the introduction of synchronized sound.

Whatever the true reason, if there was any truth or reason, Chaplin went on giving the impression of playing mute David against the noisy Goliath of the talkie. The pose looked humble but was arrogant, for Chaplin was a giant among Davids, the only major silent star who could afford to continue his personal silence. In short, Chaplin had it both ways, making a brilliant conversion to sound while claiming he intended to go on making silent pictures. Something closer to the truth is that the innately conservative Chaplin, who blamed his slowness to convert to feature-length production on his contracts (an excuse that was only partly valid), took his own time to develop an aesthetic of sound independent of the rest of the industry.

Perhaps the best way to understand the brilliance of Chaplin's initial experiment with motion picture sound is to look at and listen to *City Lights* in relation to *The Jazz Singer*. The Warner Brothers' film was a success not because it used recorded sound (many earlier films had done so—and Thomas Edison, facing market saturation for his early phonographs, had ordered his assistants to invent a motion picture device that would make existing phonographs obsolete), but because it used sound in a compelling and meaningful way. With the exception of the moment when the angry voice of the old Jewish cantor returns the film to silence, all of the sounds in *The Jazz Singer* are glorious, celebratory, for the creators of this film had asked themselves the same questions posed via the conflict between the old cantor and his jazz-singing son: to what use shall we put the gift of song—to praise God or please man? A few years later, Chaplin asked a different but equally important question: which is greater—the gift of making things heard or that of making them seen? In *City Lights*, sounds prove misleading: most spectacularly, the blind girl creates her own wonderfully false (and ultimately painful for its subject) picture of Charlie on the basis of his voice and the sound of a limousine door opening and closing. There is visual evidence of pleasant sounds (the phonograph and the canary in the blind girl's home, her pleasure in listening to Charlie), but we do not actually hear those pleasant sounds—and the "environmental" sounds we do hear are consistently unpleasant or associated with discomfort: the discordant noise of the piano when the drunken Charlie and his millionaire friend pass out and bang their heads on the keys, the sudden noise of pistol shots and sirens, the gong in the boxing ring, the piping noise of the whistle stuck in Charlie's windpipe. This last effect is a perfect example of how well Chaplin mastered sound: by letting us see and hear the way Charlie's whistling hiccups disrupt a pompous baritone's efforts to perform, Chap-

lin demonstrates that even Charlie's inadvertent noises are more enter-
taining than the best-rehearsed sounds anyone else has to offer.

Begun in 1928 and released early in 1931, *City Lights* can be traced to
a pair of projected films mentioned in a news item that appeared late in
1925: "Although it was reported that Charlie Chaplin's next picture was
to be called 'The Suicide Club,' it appears now that [Chaplin] has
virtually decided to make a comedy entitled 'The Dandy' before attack-
ing any other subject."[6] In *My Autobiography*, Chaplin explains that the
drunken millionaire subplot in *City Lights* grew out of his abandoned
"Suicide Club" project: "two members of a rich man's club, discussing
the instability of human consciousness, decide to experiment with a
tramp whom they find asleep on the [Thames] Embankment. They take
him to their palatial apartment and lavish him with wine, women and
song . . . he wakes up, thinking it has all been a dream" (A, 325). The
most important element of "The Suicide Club" retained in *City Lights* is
the notion of "the instability of human consciousness" found in the
instability of the millionaire's treatment of Charlie, in the difference
between the reality of some sounds and the conclusions that people draw
from them, and in the uncertainty or fragility of all surfaces, appearances, and arrangements. As Walter Kerr puts it, "*City Lights* is an
utterly stable film about total instability."[7] That instability is noticeable
even in the sets, for Charlie, who had strayed backward in time to the
Alaskan gold rush, is now in a kind of geographical warp, moving
through sets that include a Mediterranean ghetto, bustling American
streets, and a public park where the Star Spangled Banner is played, to a
riverside embankment that many reviewers mistook for the one beside
the Thames in London.

From Chaplin's other abandoned project, "The Dandy," comes the
notion that Charlie sees himself as an elegant gentleman of leisure.
Because of that self-image, he is able to function (albeit grotesquely) in
the world of the drunken millionaire and to enter the imagination of the
blind flower girl who "sees" in him distinguished qualities that sober
characters are blind to, qualities that Chaplin considered making visible
in a dream sequence (in *My Life in Pictures* [241], he includes a large still
of himself in an elegant white uniform and aristocratic pose).

The writing and filming of *City Lights* went on for three years, even
longer than the time taken for *The Circus*. Compared to the emotionally
chaotic conditions under which he had made his last two films, this one
was made during a period of relative personal calm—which meant he
had more energy to discharge in the film itself, more time to drive his
co-workers as never before: replacing the first actor who played the
millionaire because he would not jump into the "Thames" until the
water was warm enough to suit him, Chaplin reshot miles of film with a

new actor; growing dissatisfied with the unreliable and unprofessional Virginia Cherrill, the nearsighted amateur he had cast as the blind flower girl, he toyed with the idea of replacing her with Georgia Hale, the veteran of *The Gold Rush* with whom he was reported to be romantically linked. So great was the tension on the set that he fired Harry Crocker, his friend and assistant director.

A detailed and tantalizing glimpse into Chaplin's working habits is given by Egon Kisch, a German writer who visited Chaplin while he was editing an early version of the scene in which Charlie meets the blind girl. After screening a rough cut for Kisch and another visitor, Chaplin cross-examined them about what they had seen and became so upset when they failed to see what he wanted them to see that he invited Kisch to help him solve the problem. For eight days, Kisch remained with Chaplin, helping him to brainstorm a way to achieve the simple effect that he desired: a design that would be instantly comprehensible to every member of the audience. At the end of those eight hectic days, when Chaplin still had not arrived at the solution we can see in the finished film, Kisch reported that "the fact that the [blind] girl mistakes Charlie for the man climbing out of the automobile can in no way be grasped by the public, for it does not yet know about her blindness. This fact must therefore be revealed sooner, but [Chaplin] doesn't want to do so because he feels that the tragic discovery must be made by [Charlie] and the audience simultaneously."[8] Today, the solution Chaplin eventually arrived at seems obvious and simple: a limousine stops at the curb in front of the blind girl and Charlie, to avoid a policeman, climbs through the empty passenger compartment and steps directly into her life.

Few filmmakers—and none who worked under the assembly line methods of the big studios—had the time, resources, or even the desire to make films in this way, through trial and error. The conventional filmmaker, or even a different kind of genius (Hitchcock, for one), would have solved the visual problem before shooting any part of the film. But solutions reached on paper do not always possess the exact visual perfection of the images handcrafted through Chaplin's more empirical method.

City Lights opens with the title spelled out in lights over a shot of a city street at night. Car headlights, street lamps, and windows all contribute to the glitter as a jazzy score announces what seems to be a conventional new sound film devoted to gaiety and frivolity. With the first scene, however, we are sucked into Chaplin's very special world. It is morning and fat Henry Bergman is officiating at the dedication of a monument. When he starts to speak, he has no voice; instead, we hear what sounds like a kazoo. The joke is not so much a parody of the meaningless phrases of politicians as it is Chaplin's defiance of the new tyranny of the talkie.

The joke builds: a self-important woman gets up, then an old man with a fussy beard. They too make gibberish noises as they prepare to unveil a monument dedicated to peace and prosperity.

The monumental public unveiling at the beginning will be repeated at the end by the more personal and private "unveiling" of Charlie as the benefactor who has brought sight and prosperity to the poor blind flower girl. Thus, the dropping of the veil at the start reveals Charlie asleep in the lap of a huge stone woman. Obviously lacking in prosperity, he is awakened and given no peace by the officials who soon chase him off. Almost immediately, Charlie comes into the orbit of another female idol, the very same brazenly nude statue under which Jean Millet killed himself in A Woman of Paris. Pretending to admire other objets d'art in the window, Charlie keeps sneaking glances at the nude statue while a sidewalk elevator rises and falls behind him in token of the dangers ahead for Charlie when he dares to look upon a woman of flesh and blood.

Any doubt that this is a fully conceived sound film should be dispelled by the introduction to the shabbily dressed blind girl who now replaces the two "blind" statues. Rather than introduce her with a title identifying her by name, Chaplin employs a musical cue to begin a series of dissolves that take us from a closeup of a basket of flowers to an extreme long shot establishing the girl's relationship to the traffic on the street as a limousine pulls up at the curb. At this point, the girl seems a total non sequitur—but the dissolves and the music combine to assert her importance even before Chaplin uses a straight cut to reveal that Charlie is about to take a short cut through the limousine and into the girl's consciousness.

Note how surprised Charlie looks when the girl calls to him. Having existed on the edge of society, unnoticed except when he gets in the way, yelled at by officials, jeered by newsboys, he now finds himself being treated with the deference he probably fantasizes the world owes him. Not understanding that the girl is blind and puzzled by her politeness in the face of his obvious poverty and shabbiness, Charlie apparently concludes that the girl is so poor or so simpleminded that he seems a suitable customer to her. Acting a bit put-upon, he adopts the blasé elegance with which he inspected the art works and saunters over to choose a flower. His self-assured annoyance when she offers him the wrong flower causes him to knock another flower from her hand. After picking it up in polite reparation for his own clumsiness, he becomes extremely acerbic when she fumbles at his feet in search of the fallen flower. Raising one brow in pained response to her silliness, he tries to show her the flower and discovers she is blind. Stunned, abashed, he lets her put the flower in his lapel and pays her—but before she can give him his change, the owner of the limousine gets in and slams the door.

Always economical with camera movement, Chaplin calls attention to the owner of the limousine by panning with his briskly striding figure as he approaches the vehicle and then flash-pans back to the girl as she hears the sound of the door. Because Chaplin knows the audience can see the cause and effect relationship, he does not use a sound effect here (the absence of the sound also has the virtue of excluding us from the world of the blind girl who must rely on sound). A few seconds later, Chaplin pans with Charlie's head movement to show the limousine driving off, then pans back as Charlie turns to look at the girl as she "stares" in the direction of the departing car. Charlie, whose head movement has controlled the camera, then looks directly at the camera, as though to share his problem with us: should he correct her mistake and claim his change, or should be exploit her vulnerability by purchasing her continued esteem at some cost to himself? Charlie's solution is the same one Chaplin had made for himself about his role in this film: he keeps his silence.

But there is danger in that silence, as Charlie learns when he tiptoes away from the girl and sits down to watch her: she empties a bucket of dirty water in his face. In the next scene, trying to instill confidence and the will to live in the suicidal millionaire, Charlie speaks passionately (though all we hear is the emotional musical accompaniment) and ends up being yanked into a river at the end of a rope attached to a huge rock. Silence or speech, passive witness or active involvement, both have their danger for Charlie.

These two unexpected dousings connect the film's major subplots: Charlie's relationship to the blind girl and to the millionaire who will eventually supply Charlie with the money for the operation to restore the girl's sight. The girl and the millionaire are obviously connected in other ways: they both accept Charlie when they are in the "abnormal" state of blindness or blind-drunkenness, but when they become "normal" (that is, sighted or sober) they fail to recognize Charlie as their benefactor. Basically, Chaplin is repeating the pattern found in *The Gold Rush*, where love for a woman and friendship with a man were complexly interwoven. Like Mack Swain's Big Jim, Harry Myers's millionaire is mercurial, forgetful, threatening, and massively endearing. Charlie's love for Georgia (who also gives him a flower early on) and the blind flower girl is never consummated, but he does bed down with both Big Jim and the millionaire. In *City Lights*, however, the millionaire seems not only an extension of Charlie (note the similar mustaches, the identical tuxedoes, and the millionaire's confusion about whether he or

Charlie is driving a careening Rolls Royce) but a projection of the
Chaplin described by the wives, mistresses, friends, and children who
wrote of his moodiness, of the difficulty of knowing from day to day what
to expect of him. "Enjoy any Charlie Chaplin you have the good luck or
chance to encounter," Max Eastman warned, explaining why he could
not take seriously Chaplin's suggestion that they collaborate on a script.
"But don't try to link them up to anything you can grasp. There are too
many of them. The one that wants to collaborate with me . . . I doubt if
he lives through the night."[9] So with Chaplin's millionaire alter ego: he
is a friend who cannot last through the night.

Once the basic premises are established—that the girl is blind, that
she thinks Charlie is rich, and that the millionaire knows and loves
Charlie only when he is drunk—the remainder of the film elaborates
upon the comic and romantic potentials of those premises. Charlie's
various schemes for raising money to help the girl, the comic indignities
he suffers at her hands because of her blindness, the off-and-on again
affections of the millionaire—all provide endless opportunity for gags.
Chaplin's problem, of course, was how to bring an end to the laughs and
escape, with some dignity and acclaim, from the mechanical contrivance
he had built for himself. The escape begins with the sequence in which
all three premises flow together: after giving Charlie a wad of bills to pay
for the operation that restores the girl's sight, the millionaire sobers up
and has Charlie arrested and sent to prison.

The formal ending of the film begins as the girl turns from the flowers
she is arranging in the elegant shop she now seems to manage or own and
looks into a mirror to check her hairdo. It is unnecessary to ask how or
why she has become so prosperous in the three seasons that have passed
since Charlie was taken away to prison, for sight is a precious gift and
bears tangible benefits. But her material prosperity, like the physical gift
of vision, has not brought the peace to which the monument was
dedicated, for she is unhappy that her mysterious, remote, godlike
benefactor has not revealed himself to her. Having placed the girl in the
same symbolic position at the end of the film as the crowd awaiting the
unveiling of the monument at the start, Chaplin reverses the order and
direction of Charlie's first trip through the city: Charlie looks for the girl
at her old corner, passes without a glance the shop where he once
admired the nude statue, and is again mocked by the newsboys. The
final unveiling begins when one of the newsboys yanks on the piece of
fabric poking through the hole torn in the seat of Charlie's trousers by
the sword of one of the monumental figures at the start. In her shop, the
girl laughs at the sight of the tramp's furious reaction to his tormentors
and at the practical but uncouth use to which he puts the rag yanked
from his trousers: he blows his nose on it before tucking it away like a

dandy's neatly folded handkerchief. The girl laughs because she has just seen a monumental figure enjoyed by millions of people around the world since 1914: Charlie the character and Chaplin the artist. Up to this point, the "unveiling" scene has been photographed from the neutral point of view of the street, Charlie in the foreground, the girl in the background on the other side of a plate glass window that separates Charlie from his "creation" just as another shop window separated Charlie from the nude statue crafted by another artist. But as Charlie begins to turn toward the window behind him, Chaplin cuts to a reverse angle over the shoulder of the girl in order to show us what she sees on her personal screen. To prepare us for the next stage in the unveiling, Chaplin imposes four or five seconds of dead silence on the soundtrack as Charlie completes the turn and recognizes the girl. When the heart-rending music resumes, petals begin to drop from the discarded flower Charlie recovered from the gutter. Noticing the sad condition of his flower, she offers him a fresh one, thus repeating the initial offer that resulted in such pain and pleasure for Charlie.

This new offer panics him for reasons that are left unclear. Is it that he does not want to ruin her romantic image of him—or is he afraid of his beautiful creation? Whatever the reason, he scuttles away until she stops him with her voice. Not until she puts a coin in his hand, thus returning as casual charity the earlier offering he could little afford, does she begin to know what her eyes could never tell her. Closing his hand around the coin, she begins to feel the truth she cannot see as her right hand retraces its old path to the lapel where she put that first flower so long before.

Of the famous final closeup of Charlie framed against a suddenly darkened background by the glowing nimbus of the girl's hair, Chaplin makes a claim he makes about no other scene: "I had had several takes and they were all overdone, overacted, overfelt. This time I was looking more at [the actress], interested to see that she didn't make any mistakes. It was a beautiful sensation of not acting, of standing outside myself."[10] In that final closeup, then, Charlie and Chaplin are one and the same, Pygmalions looking at their Galateas, artists admiring what they have wrought.

Modern Times—Chaplin in the Vast Machine

City Lights brought Chaplin the kind of adulation he had not known since *The Kid.* Many considered it his greatest achievement—and Albert Einstein got teary-eyed at the premiere. Taking a well-deserved rest, Chaplin shut down his studio and embarked on a fifteen-month world tour during which he claimed membership in the twentieth century's most exalted and exclusive club: he met Churchill and Gandhi, argued with Shaw, and enjoyed a first-name acquaintance with a future king of England. There was talk that he would produce a film entitled "London" on location—and rumors that he would be knighted. In Europe, there were numerous honors and a torrid affair with a young woman named May Reeves.[11] After narrowly escaping an assassination plot that took the life of the prime minister of Japan, he returned to California in the summer of 1932 and dictated *A Comedian Sees the World*, an account of his meetings with world leaders and his opinions on the economic, social, and political crises facing mankind. Looking for a story that would allow him some scope for his now-overt ambitions as a world-class philosopher, he struggled for more than a year before announcing plans for a new film in August of 1933: it would employ pantomime rather than speech, would be set in a factory area, and would star his new discovery, Paulette Goddard, who had already played small parts at one of the major studios. A month later he announced the reopening of his studio—but another year passed before the major photography began. Not until early 1935, more than four years after the release of *City Lights*, did the still-unfinished "Production No. 5" have a definite title: "The Masses."

The heavy social and political connotations of that title were reflected in the summary of the film Chaplin gave to a reporter: on his way home from the factory after being fired, Charlie would hitch a ride on the back of a truck. When the danger flag fell from the truck, he would get down, pick it up, run after the truck, and be arrested as an agitator. The film would then build toward a final rally, presumably of the unemployed or disaffected.[12] At this stage, eleven months before the film was released, Chaplin was apparently thinking of having Charlie accidentally become a symbol (and, perhaps, a leader) of the masses and of ending the film as he would end *The Great Dictator*, where Charlie's Tomanian avatar is thrust into the position of giving an inspirational speech before a huge crowd.

Ultimately, Chaplin backed away from the politically oriented title and theme and from connecting Charlie to the masses of humanity; instead, he elected to place Charlie in the more neutral setting indicated by the title under which the film was finally released in early 1936, *Modern Times*. This title is a bit of a come-on, for there was nothing particularly modern or novel about the times Chaplin was depicting—at least not for Chaplin, who had been dealing with the themes of hunger, poverty, unemployment, and homelessness for twenty years. Partly because of the press releases and rumors about the contemporary nature of the film, many American critics and viewers mistakenly expected the new film to be an expression of Chaplin's solidarity with the masses.

They were, however, puzzled and sometimes angered by the political and social implications of the finished product in which Charlie stands against everything and everyone other than the Gamine played by Paulette Goddard. Berserk on the assembly line, he squirts management and labor alike with an oil can that sometimes seems to spring from his crotch ("piss on both sides," he seems to be saying); in prison, he does not so much prevent a jail break as protect himself against other prisoners; when his new co-workers go on strike, Charlie is visibly annoyed and disappointed; as a waiter, he makes life hard for the other waiters by going through the wrong door; whereas the other waiters sing together in harmony, Charlie performs solo in a language known, if at all, only to himself.

There is no simple or single reason for the unprecedented five-year hiatus between *City Lights* and its successor. In addition to the confusion about the focus (was it to be about "The Street Waif" of one early title, Charlie, or the masses?), the production was very expensive, demanding a waterfront district and a huge factory set with monstrous moving props. And then there was the difficulty brought on by Chaplin's continued resistance to the conventions of sound. On the eve of the New York premiere of *City Lights*, he had told Mordaunt Hall that though he "might direct and produce a talking picture in which he did not act," he would never appear in one.[13] Even during his long vacation abroad, the thought of making a new silent picture had left him "obsessed by a depressing fear of being old-fashioned," while the idea of a talkie "sickened me, for I realized I could never achieve the excellence of my silent pictures. It would mean giving up my tramp character entirely. Some people suggested that the tramp might talk. This was unthinkable, for the first word he ever uttered would transform him into another person" (*A*, 366). After his return to Hollywood, he claims to have considered retiring from the screen entirely rather than make a choice between giving in to sound or fighting back. Eventually, he compromised by making an even more elaborate sound picture than before while insisting that it was silent. By and large, his major critics and biographers have accepted the claim and refer to *Modern Times* with varying degrees of inadequate or inaccurate qualification as "a silent film," "a true silent film," "silent save for music and effects," and "technically . . . in effect a silent film, except for the ironic gibberish Charlie sang at the end."[14] In spite of substantial use of the human voice (on a record, over loudspeakers, in crowd noises, and in two songs), in spite of funny sound effects and of scenes shot "wild" and edited to theme music as playful as any we find in the films of the French New Wave, *Modern Times* is still sometimes thought of or remembered as having been a totally silent film. Peter Cotes, for instance, speaks of Chaplin writing "music for the revised *Modern Times* when it was revived . . . with a sound accompaniment several years ago."[15]

Far from being silent, *Modern Times* is a very satisfactory continuation of Chaplin's careful exploration of the possibilities of sound. Anyone who still thinks that *Modern Times* is a silent film, or even "essentially" a silent film, should watch it with the sound turned off or should see the rare silent version in which intertitles replace audible dialogue.[16] Great parts of the film become literally meaningless or emotionally ambiguous. A true silent film must make sense and move us as the creator intends without the help of any sound. *Modern Times* simply does not pass the test of silence.

Perhaps significantly, the first words of the film that Chaplin made so slowly under the working title of "Production No. 5" are "Section five. Speed her up." And those words are spoken by Allan Garcia, the same actor who had played the cruel ringmaster in *The Circus*. Just as the circus film provided an opportunity to comment covertly on the nature of filmmaking, so the opening of *Modern Times* provides a beautifully worked-out allegorical commentary on Chaplin's craft. Chaplin told a reporter that before he began *Modern Times* he had "wondered what would happen to the progress of the mechanical age if one person decided to act like a bull in a china shop. . . . I decided it would make a good story to take a little man and make him thumb his nose at all the recognized rules and conventions."[17] Though this statement was made at the time the film came out, it bears little specific relevance to the content of *Modern Times*, for by no stretch of the imagination does Charlie "thumb his nose at all recognized rules and conventions." Rather, it is Chaplin who, as we shall see, cocked a snook at a few of the rules and conventions of the industrial system and mechanical process he knew best, the motion pictures.

This hypothesis can be tested against the foreword that has puzzled and annoyed some viewers: "'Modern Times.' A story of industry, of individual enterprise—humanity crusading in the pursuit of happiness." For "industry," read "the film industry"; for "humanity," read "Chaplin." Those crowds of sheep and workers who appear immediately after the foreword are, metaphorically (and in the case of the human "extras," literally), the rank and file of the factory system Chaplin had labored in for more than twenty years. The self-referential nature of the opening begins to assert itself through the single black sheep that stands out in the middle of the flock like Chaplin's mustache in the middle of his white face—and becomes clearer in the scene that begins immediately after the thematic montage that suggests factory workers act like sheep: we see a handsome Adonis figure throw a switch to start up the factory and Chaplin cuts to the office of his alter ego, the boss played by Allan

Garcia. This worthy gentleman sits in dead silence, fiddling with a jigsaw puzzle, then picks up the Sunday comics, and finally gulps down a pill before turning on the machinery that both captures and projects his voice and image. Up to this point, there has been nothing particularly amusing outside the contrast between the masses of humanity rushing to work and the bored executive who seems to have trouble concentrating on his childish tasks, tasks not unlike those of Chaplin who put together his own comic jigsaw puzzles and called them movies. But as soon as the boss orders a speed-up for section five, a rapid process of editing and camera movement takes us to the person who is holding up production in this factory, Charlie—who is played, of course, by the person who held up production in the Chaplin fun-works. Look again at the assembly line Charlie is working on: the little squares of metal moving on the belt in front of him resemble the individual frames in a piece of film. And the machine into which the "frames" (and Charlie) disappear looks suspiciously like the innards of a camera or a projector.

Thus, the opening is a playful commentary on the internal and external pressures upon Chaplin to keep up his level of productivity, to keep the films moving on his own assembly line. Consider the announcement Chaplin made about his production plans in the summer of 1935, when he was editing *Modern Times:* he would produce and direct six features in the next two years, two starring himself and Paulette Goddard, two starring Goddard, and two starring others.[18] There was a kind of self-deceptive madness in such a boast, the desperation of the hapless victim Waldo Frank had glimpsed a decade earlier when he asserted that Chaplin "is caught in a vast machine which he has created and which he does not run."[19] We begin to see the shape of that machine in the contrast between Chaplin's two alter egos: the taskmaster boss who lusts after more product and poor Charlie, who cannot keep up the pace without cracking.

What had slowed Chaplin down most, of course, were the problems associated with making a sound picture (the greater need for preplanning and scripting, the attendant loss in spontaneity), problems that were compounded by the fact that he clung to silent techniques: because the new film was not totally in the silent or sound camp, Chaplin had to spend many extra months reconciling the contrasting methods of style and narrative development peculiar to the silent and sound eras. True, he had faced similar problems in making *City Lights*, but that film had not been a "talkie." Chaplin's antagonism toward the conventions of the talkie is vented early in his new film through the use and abuse of the human voice. Though we hear "live" singing and shouting near the end of the film, by which time Chaplin seems to have come to personal terms with sound, at the start the human voice exists only as a mechanically broadcast or recorded medium of oppression or exploitation. For instance, it is a mechanically recorded voice that introduces the most outrageous (and comic) of the demons that torment poor Charlie: the feeding machine. "Actions speak louder than words," boasts the prerecorded sales pitch, a piece of industrial poetry that stands up to comparison with W. H. Auden's "The Unknown Citizen." Actions do indeed speak louder than words in this film, but the words themselves are necessary on the soundtrack to help the audience bridge the huge distance between the inventor's concept and the reality, a gap that parallels that between Chaplin's press releases and the movie itself. We must hear the voice tout the feeding machine's "aerodynamic, streamlined body" while we look upon its unlovely form and wonder what possible aim could be served by streamlining a feeding machine.

Chaplin's opening montage and the Rube Goldberg narrative machinery leading up to the discovery of Charlie at work are mirrored in the feeding machine, for the whole opening sequence is the cinematic equivalent of a feeding machine, a busy, clanking, mechanical, efficient, and most un-Chaplinesque force-feeding of images. Not until Chaplin appears as Charlie are we allowed to savor and digest the comic and human sustenance of the main course Chaplin puts in front of us.

For an appetizer, we have the conceit that Charlie cannot stop tightening nuts when he steps away from the assembly line to take a break. He twitches mechanically for several seconds until he is able to shake himself back into something approximating human form. There is a literal soup course when the line shuts down for lunch: Charlie seems to be able to move normally until he picks up his co-worker's soup bowl and jerks it empty. The main course, so to speak, comes when the boss tests the feeding machine on Charlie, who is forced to eat parts of the machine. Then there is a second main course during which Charlie is "eaten" by the machine he is supposed to feed with components. Having passed through the bowels of the machine, he is regurgitated in time for a nutty desert: moving with extreme grace and precision rather than in jerks and jitters, he tries to tighten the noses, nipples, and buttons of men and women alike, causes the boss's audiovisual equipment to go on the blink, and oils the boss and his henchmen as though they are a bunch of sick machines.

Just as the first three scenes in *City Lights* (that is, those before the meeting with the drunken millionaire) seem the most fully realized and thematically coherent, so too with the long opening sequence in the factory. It amounts to seventeen and a half of the film's eighty-five minutes—a mere fifth—and when it is over the best part of the film has ended for many critics. Even the generally admiring and tolerant Theodore Huff is unhappy about the structure of the remainder of *Modern*

Times: "There is fuzziness in the form, drag in the pace, breaks in the continuity, and lack of climax. The last [four-fifths] of the picture is a sort of an anticlimax to the opening idea."[20] The problem, it would seem, is that most critics want the film to continue along the mechanical lines of the opening sequence. When Huff speaks of "drag in the pace, breaks in the continuity," he is turning the film into an out-of-order extension of the feeding machine with its "synchromesh transmission." The genius of *Modern Times* is not that it is as slickly crafted and tightly designed as *The Gold Rush* but that it has an organic form: what Huff mistakes for "fuzziness" is the natural outline of the living narrative.

Putting aside, then, any hankering after a rigid formal structure, let us turn back to the exact point at which the gag machine seems to fly apart. Released from a hospital after being cured of the nervous breakdown brought on by the pressures of the assembly line, Charlie picks up a danger flag that has fallen from the back of a passing truck and is mistakenly arrested as a Communist agitator after a mob of demonstrators turns the corner in back of him. The whole episode, from the time of his release from the hospital to the pulling away of the paddy wagon, takes a total of about ninety seconds. The speed is important: though the gag seems to have originally been intended to involve Charlie in the political destinies of the masses, Chaplin rushes through it to get Charlie off the street and into a prison that echoes the regimentation of the factory. But instead of cutting directly to the prison scene, Chaplin immediately and surprisingly introduces a new character: "The gamine—a child of the waterfront, who refuses to go hungry."

Although the Gamine and the particular form of her stubbornness may seem to be non sequiturs at first, close examination of the film reveals that food and the act of eating provides an informal focus or motivation for nearly every major scene or sequence until the very end. As the film develops, access to food becomes increasingly easy and hunger less pressing, so that in the long restaurant scene, the hunger of Charlie and the Gamine is no longer an issue and the hunger theme has been reduced to a joke about a well-dressed gentleman who is annoyed at having to wait for his dinner, an entire roast duck.

Of all Chaplin's hungry characters, the Gamine is the most voracious. When we first see her, she is stealing and eating bananas on the waterfront. Chaplin undercranks the action to suggest her efficiency as an organism for gathering and consuming food. With a knife clasped in her gleaming teeth, she looks and acts like a manic pirate—like a female incarnation of Doug Fairbanks, whose career had gone into decline. Indeed, Chaplin seems to have cherished Paulette Goddard for the playfulness and companionship he found in Fairbanks. Divorced at the time Chaplin met her, the twenty-year-old Goddard moved into the

Chaplin mansion and soon turned it into the first genuine home Chaplin
had ever enjoyed. She changed things around, introduced Chaplin to
new foods, controlled the servants, became a beloved and loving companion and surrogate mother to Chaplin's two young sons, stayed on
good terms with their alcoholic and troubled mother, and kept Chaplin
active with sailing and tennis.

The playful yet mature relationship between Chaplin and Goddard is
reflected in *Modern Times*. Charlie's attraction to the Gamine is allowed
to develop slowly and realistically—as was Chaplin's personal relationship to Goddard (it took them about four years to marry). There is, in this
film, no sudden and overwhelming explosion of love or passion—and the
course of true love will run slower and slower in succeeding films. Most
importantly in *Modern Times*, the relationship between Charlie and the
girl, like that between Chaplin and the actress, is mutually supportive.
Look at the scene in which Charlie and the Gamine sit down to rest after
escaping from the police van. It is obvious that Charlie (or Chaplin) is
interested in what the girl is saying—not simply in the girl. He thinks
about her responses, making a doubtful face at one point. His mind, not
just his heart, is engaged. For these modern times, Chaplin supplied his
first modern romance.

Although Chaplin enjoyed a relatively stable personal life with Goddard, Charlie's world remained as shifty as before. He starts out as a
factory worker, but loses his job. He finally gets it back, but the union
goes on strike. He likes prison, but he is paroled. He tries to return to
prison, but is recaptured by the girl. He writes a song on his cuffs, but
loses the cuffs. He finally has a steady job, but has to move on. Mutabil-
ity is both the medium and the message. The "total instability" that
Walter Kerr admired in the content of the "utterly stable" *City Lights*
has become an organizing principle.

The apparent lack of order and consistency does not, however, mean
that the film is actually disorganized in any way. To the contrary, its
sudden shifts in tone and apparent contradictions or digressions, easily
mistaken for a machine going out of order, can more appropriately be
seen to resemble a growing plant, branching out to seek the sun in one
direction while rooting down into the soil for moisture and nutrients.
Consider the resulting photo(play)synthesis of the contrasting content
and style of the stories of Charlie and the Gamine before they come
together. The Gamine's father, like Charlie, is unemployed—but Charlie's unemployment leads to comic misadventures, the father's to
hunger, shame, depression, and death. When someone shoots at Charlie, we laugh; in the very next scene, there is nothing funny about the
shots that kill the Gamine's father. The attempted prison break is played
for laughs, but the Gamine's successful escape from the authorities who
come to collect her and her orphaned sisters is melodramatic. Her

escape is a sign that she values absolute freedom (even to be homeless and hungry) above the confining welfare of the state, the welfare Charlie has already firmly embraced by the time we cut back to him in his cosy new cell. At this point, Charlie and the Gamine are worlds apart, on opposite sides of the newspaper Charlie is reading. "STRIKES AND RIOTS!," scream the headlines, "BREADLINES BROKEN BY UNRULY MOB." Charlie reads those headlines and shakes his head with the blasé disapproval of someone who has it made.

Even when Charlie and the Gamine finally meet, they are still far apart in terms of the way they look at the world—and the style of Chaplin's treatment of them. She has stolen a loaf of bread—a "crime" that is realistic in motive and commission. Trying and failing to take the blame for her crime so he can get back to prison, Charlie promptly forgets her and comically escalates her modest crime by wolfing down enough delicacies to feed a family for a week. Meeting the Gamine again in a paddy wagon, he is nothing more than polite until a sudden narrative turn (and her fierce determination to remain free) throws them out onto the street together. Learning of her hunger and homelessness, he fantasizes what it would be like to have an idyllic suburban home where food grows on the trees and a self-milking cow makes home deliveries. When his daydream ends, she still bears the sensory weight of reality: she feels the pangs of hunger and sees the cop who causes them to move on. And she is equally realistic when she learns a watchman has been injured on the job: whereas others stand idly by, she sends Charlie in to apply for the post. Once she is fed, Charlie's fantasies take over again: he leads her to the toy department where he dons skates for a graceful ballet, then dresses her in fur and puts her to bed in a display of elegant furniture.

From the time the Gamine steals that loaf of bread, all of the occasions for comedy, grace, and fantasy grow out of her specific and realistic needs for food and shelter, needs that are the air, soil, and water in which the comic plant grows under the solar furnace of Chaplin's genius. The narrative "fruit" of this growth is that the initially realistic and humorless Gamine becomes infected with Charlie's visionary abilities. On the day they meet, he not only daydreams about their having a home together but tries to turn a whole department store into a home; when he gets out of jail after that fiasco, she leads him to a tumbledown shack she has fixed up. Though the shack assaults him with falling lumber and threatens to collapse around him, he cherishes it as part of her dream and does nothing to discourage her attempt to make real the idyllic domestic daydream he described on the day they met. In his daydream cottage, she was cooking pork chops for dinner when he returned from work; in her waking version of his dream, she cooks him a breakfast of ham steak before he sets out for his new factory job with the promise he will earn them a "real" home. The first time they met, she had stared in amazement as Charlie lied about who stole the bread; toward the end, it is his turn to be amazed when she lies about his qualifications to get him a job as a singing waiter.

Just as Charlie and the Gamine eventually merge, Charlie and Chaplin converge in the song toward which the comic and romantic action builds. The two halves of the artist had been separated ever since the outset, when the alter ego factory boss spoke the first words ever heard in a Chaplin film to decree the speed up. Imagine the situation in 1936 as the imaginary and real audiences waited impatiently in the cabaret on the screen and in movie houses around the world for the stage-shy Charlie and the mike-shy Chaplin to stop delaying the inevitable moment at which they open their common mouth and utter . . . nonsense. Occupying the same place in *Modern Times* as the tilting cabin in *The Gold Rush*, the high-wire act in *The Circus*, the "cuff-song" is a show-stopping physical performance that follows upon carefully constructed suspense about whether or not our hero can bring it off.

Chaplin brings it off brilliantly, of course, employing a lush blend of fake romance languages (as in his next film he will stir together a potpourri of pseudo-Teutonic grunts and growls). But when he stops the show in the cabaret, the show on the screen continues, for the instant the song is over and Charlie has returned to the Gamine in the dressing room, Chaplin reverts joyously and without transition to the faster motion of silent comedy even though we can hear the "realistic" sound of the unseen audience laughing, cheering, and applauding.

Once Charlie has sung his song—and Chaplin broken his long personal silence—*Modern Times* rushes to its powerful final shot: the image of Charlie and the Gamine walking up the road together toward the sunrise. Though that image is quite successful and satisfying on the iconographic and sentimental levels, it still needs to be considered in relation to the method and movement of the entire film and to the social and economic conditions that inspired the film. Perhaps the best way to understand what Chaplin has achieved in that final scene is to compare it to the end of another classic film that grew out of the Great Depression, John Ford's *The Grapes of Wrath* (1940). Charlie's final speech to the Gamine ("Buck up—never say die! We'll get along") obviously resembles Ma Joad's final optimism as the family moves on. But everything that has come before is different. The Joads keep moving forward endlessly from start to finish, but Charlie has been going around in circles from the beginning—or, to put it more exactly, his narrative course describes one great circle and begins to describe a second until the circle is formally broken at the end.

The first great circle takes us from the beginning (the factory workers flowing to their jobs) to the awakening of Charlie and the Gamine on the dawn of Charlie's new factory job. That new job comes within the emotional and narrative logic of the film in such a way that it seems a synthesis of Charlie's grandiose imaginings and the Gamine's ability to find realistic solutions to their needs. That is, of course, the same synthesis supplied by FDR's New Deal: a vision of what could be done and a practical understanding of how to do it. Thus, when Charlie sits down to breakfast in their modest "home" and opens the paper, he reads headlines proclaiming metaphorically that "PROSPERITY HAS TURNED THE CORNER" and literally that factories are reopening.

But Chaplin was no publicist for the New Deal—and Charlie soon finds that the nightmare is not over, that he has simply returned to his starting point. He had lost his first factory job because he cracked under management's dream of increased productivity. Now it is labor's dream of increased wages and benefits, shorter hours, or raw power (the exact reason for the strike is not stated) that sends him back out into the streets where the cops are waiting. It is all a crazy merry-go-round—and both Charlie and Chaplin need to find a way to get off. For both, the escape comes via the grand finale of the cabaret scene in which Chaplin mimics the frenzy of the first factory scene and discharges all of the kinetic and emotional energy the film has been storing up ever since the power got turned on by the big switch-tender at the start.

This final sequence begins, immediately after Charlie's last arrest, with a shot of a literal merry-go-round that objectifies the mad revolutions of plot and fortune. Panning from the merry-go-round, Chaplin reveals the Gamine twirling around and around in the street. A few seconds later, he dissolves from her dancing in the street wearing a ragged black dress to her dancing in the cabaret wearing a sparkling costume. Granted that the image is, in and of itself, gay and appealing, it is, within the context of the film, as emblematic of dancing to someone else's tune as Charlie's performance on the assembly line at the start. At the end of *Modern Times*, Charlie has enough energy to carry the girl with him into the "outer" space of the long, straight road that stretches away toward the distant horizon and the sunrise. Free of assembly lines and impersonal social processes at last, they have finally escaped the vast machine.

5

The Doomed Tyrant

Finding a New Persona: *The Great Dictator*

THOUGH CHAPLIN may not have known it when he shot the final scene in *Modern Times,* the image of Charlie tramping up the road with the Gamine was to mark the last appearance of the lonely little outcast he had developed over a period of more than twenty years. Chaplin would wear a clean, neat version of the "tramp" costume in his next film, but the man inside the costume has a job, a home, a nationality, a religion, a place in the world, and a voice. It is that voice, more than anything else, that sets the little Jewish barber apart from Charlie.

Returning to Hollywood in mid-1936 after a long cruise in the Pacific, Chaplin was faced again with having to decide whether or not Charlie would speak in his next film. After agonizing for more than a year, Chaplin finally announced late in 1937 that he would never again play the tramp figure known as Charlie and would make his new screen debut in a talking role within a year.[1] Few could have suspected then that Chaplin's career behind and in front of the camera had not even reached its chronological midpoint. Many simply assumed that the last holdover from the pioneering decades was going the way of the other founders of United Artists—Pickford, Fairbanks, and Griffith—who had all ended their careers except for futile attempts at comebacks. For a while, Chaplin considered retiring from the screen temporarily in order to build a film around Paulette Goddard. With Goddard in mind, he bought the rights to D. L. Murray's *Regency,* a fat historical novel tracing the lives of five generations of rebellious, independent women. He also toyed with the idea of starring Goddard in a talkie remake of *A Woman of Paris* or in *White Russian,* the original script that eventually became his final film, *A Countess from Hong Kong.*

Coming on the heels of the abdication of Edward VIII, the apparent capitulation of Charlie occasioned editorial comment in the *New York Times:* "It is an ironical thought that the mustached face of Adolf Hitler will be the only living reminder of the little clown. Good-bye, Charlot. Pleasant dreams."[2] Even more ironical was that the editorial writer did not know that Chaplin had just received or was about to receive a suggestion that he play both parts in "a Hitler story based on mistaken identity" (A, 391). Though he claims to have dismissed the idea at first, he eventually saw the dual role as a solution to the problem of how he could speak on screen: "As Hitler I could harangue the crowds in jargon and talk all I wanted to. And as the tramp I could remain more or less silent. A Hitler story was an opportunity for burlesque and pantomime" (A, 392). A Hitler story also meant he could keep his trademark mustache.

Finally, a Hitler parody would allow him to return to a theme that had first interested him as early as 1932, when he told a reporter in Singapore that his next picture "might be about the world crisis." The *New York Times* had editorialized favorably on that notion, proclaiming that Chaplin might "enliven the whole world with a caricature of its worries" by chosing "the role of reformer, dictator, savior of the world."[3] By the time he had finished *Modern Times*, the world crisis had taken on a convenient triple focus that proved ideal for Chaplin's comic purposes: Fascism, Germany, and Hitler. "Ve haf vays of may-kink you talk," the typical Nazi interrogator sneers in the movies. Hitler made Chaplin talk—and gave him something to talk about.

With the decision to burlesque Hitler, Chaplin launched a trilogy of films that would take fourteen years to complete: *The Great Dictator*, *Monsieur Verdoux*, and *Limelight*. In all three films, he plays multiple roles (the Dictator and the Barber, Verdoux as he "really" is and as he pretends to be, and Calvero sober or drunk, awake or in his dreams, off the stage or before an audience). In each film, he plays a doomed, tyrannical figure who moves toward death. And when the trilogy was completed by the death of Calvero, the gentlest of tyrants, Chaplin's Hollywood career came to its end.

Though Chaplin rarely admitted being influenced by others in his selection of characters or stories, he was careful to note that the idea of playing moral monsters in *The Great Dictator* and *Monsieur Verdoux* came from others rather than from within. Given Chaplin's extreme reluctance to share credit for anything, his generosity in these two cases should set off warning signals: the old con man is up to his tricks because he does not want to admit to himself (or allow us to see) from how deep within himself Adenoid Hynkel and Henri Verdoux have come. Only in *Limelight*, for which he shares no credit, does he admit that Calvero and Chaplin are cut from the same motley cloth.

Chaplin's desire to satirize Hitler probably came from the same source as his fascination with the idea of playing Napoleon; less obviously, the Hitler role represents the abandonment of the persona behind which

Chaplin had hidden for so long. Perhaps because he saw the danger in coming directly into the open, Chaplin ended up relying on the humble figure of the Barber as an emotional and narrative stand-in. We see the Barber as a soldier in World War I before we see the Dictator; we later see him wearing what looks like Charlie's typical costume; we finally see him wearing Hynkel's uniform. But let us not be fooled: the movie is entitled *The Great Dictator*, the word "dictator" or "dictators" was in every working title, and it is the figure of Adenoid Hynkel we remember when we think of this film.

And that is as it should be, for Hitler supplied Chaplin with an opportunity to look at himself as man and artist while pretending to be looking at someone else. Late in life, Chaplin told Lillian Ross that "when I first saw Hitler, with that little mustache, I thought he was copying *me*, taking advantage of my success. I was that egotistical."[4] One can imagine Hitler making the same egotistical mistake about Chaplin.

Although Roger Manvell, who (like Robert Payne) wrote biographies of both Chaplin and Hitler, insists that "the resemblance . . . stopped short at the mustache,"[5] the similarities between the great director and the great dictator are astonishing. Born a mere four days and six hundred miles apart to drunken fathers and worshipped mothers, each grew up ashamed of early poverty and family histories of madness and illegitimacy; each saw his life story as a process of constant struggle; fascinated by Napoleon and Christ, each longed to play him in his own way; attracted romantically to a string of teenaged girls, each married motion picture actresses; each established his power base in 1919 (the year that marked the founding of United Artists and the Nazi party); obsessively perfectionist, each sulked or raged and otherwise acted like a spoiled child when he did not get his way; each loved music and used it in his work; each was a master of costume and set design. Surrounded like Chaplin by sycophants and favored henchmen of little talent, Hitler tried to wage war the way Chaplin made movies—by making all decisions himself, often in prolonged solitude while his lieutenants and the world waited. Like Hitler, Chaplin had erratic work habits and expected everyone else to come to the studio just in case he decided to show up. People close to both recount their constant petty duplicity: smiling and agreeing with visitors, sneering at the visitors when they were gone. Vindictive and cruel one moment, they were equally capricious and surprising in their kindness and consideration. Their economic, political, and social philosophies were confused and confusing, though Hitler was probably the more consistent.

It is sometimes difficult to tell whether a statement was made by or about Hitler or Chaplin. Waldo Frank's description of Chaplin's reaction to grisly photographs of Chinese tortures and executions sounds like the rantings of Hitler: "Suddenly his eyes hardened; he jumped up, and his mouth was cruel. 'There's humanity for you! By God, they deserve it. Give it to them! That's man. Cut 'em up. Torture 'em! The bastards!'"[6] The comments of others who knew Chaplin well could be just as easily mistaken for assertions about Hitler: "Brooding for hours at a time, untrained and illogical, the poisoned weeds of a frustrated childhood had grown rank in his mind"; "He has no unity of character, no principles or convictions, nothing in his head that, when he lays it on the pillow, you can sensibly expect will be there in the morning."[7]

Conversely, the Chaplin scholar who reads Robert G. L. Waite's massive biography of Hitler will be startled by the familiarity of many passages. "He forgot—or failed to tell the truth about—generally known facts of his personal life"; "'In retrospect, I am completely uncertain when and where he was ever really himself, his image not distorted by play acting'"; "The fact that he had no conception of musical composition . . . did not deter him. His genius, he said, would surmount any difficulty. 'I shall compose the music,' he said to a friend, 'and you will write it down'"; "his favorite diversion was movies . . . an effective actor and an excellent mimic, he worked up routines"; "Hitler was a lethargic person who frittered away thousands of working hours in idle self-indulgence. Day after day and in all night sessions he forced his associates to listen to interminable and empty dissertations on trivia."[8] (Compare a Chaplin biographer: "Chaplin will stay up all night, walking the length of his living room, gesticulating forcefully, talking volubly on a subject about which he knows practically nothing.")[9]

To be sure, there were important differences: one feared that he might be part Jewish, the other hoped and boasted that he was; one never danced, the other never missed an opportunity to show his grace. Childless Hitler seemed genuinely to like children but was responsible for the death of millions; Chaplin professed to hate children but sired nearly a dozen that we know of.

Out of these endless similarities and contrasts comes one crucial point: Hitler provided Chaplin with highly personal elements of attraction and repulsion. It is irrelevant whether or not he was aware of the self-referential nature of his parody of Hitler, whose voice and movements he studied in newsreels; irrelevant whether or not he perceived that Charlie and Hitler were very much alike: lonely, outcast guttersnipes, misunderstood and persecuted by authority, shy around women, insanely optimistic, infinitely photogenic, and relentlessly determined to reshape the world to their own needs.

Once he had decided to burlesque Hitler, Chaplin spent close to two years developing the story. In late 1938, several months before he finally began writing the script, the first rumors reached the press: "Charlie

Chaplin will talk in his next picture, in which he will play the role of a prisoner in a concentration camp, but because he can't speak his fellow-prisoners' language the talk will be all jargon, aided by Chaplinesque pantomime."[10] A month later, it was known the work in progress was called "The Dictator" and was being attacked by the German press; within another few months, it was rumored that Chaplin had added a parody of Mussolini and was calling his project "The Dictators." Though rumors continued to appear about the plot of the new film, tight secrecy closed down around the project while Chaplin went through several scripts. Shooting began on 9 September 1939, a week after Germany invaded Poland and the French and British declared war. What had seemed a clever topic for a comedy had become a potential liability with a grandiose title: "The Great Dictator."

Ignoring warnings that Hitler was no subject for humor, Chaplin plunged ahead as only the complete master of a studio could, spending his own money to create an entire nation. He gave it a name (spelt variously as Tomainia or Tomania) that combined "ptomaine" and "mania," invented a language (spoken only by Hynkel and Field Marshall Herring), and designed uniforms and icons (the sign of the "double cross" in place of the swastika) and a national style in public art (Venus de Milo and Rodin's Thinker giving straight arm salutes). He gave his fictional nation neighbors (the helpless Osterlich and the aggressive Bacteria) and built an elaborate ghetto set.

To flesh out his imaginary world, Chaplin assembled his most effective and varied cast. Very few of Chaplin's old-timers appear—Hank Mann, Leo White, and Chester Conklin have small parts, but even the faithful Henry Bergman is nowhere to be seen—for when one sets out to invade a new territory, even if it is only the alien landscape of the full-scale talkie, one recruits the best professionals available. As Hannah, Paulette Goddard brought experience gained in more than half a dozen films under other directors. Filling the same basic function in the "palace" scenes as does Hannah in the ghetto was Henry Daniell's epicine Garbitsch, the tough-minded, manipulative minister of propaganda who eggs Hynkel on as Hannah eggs on the Barber. Chaplin's scenes with Daniell are unlike any other in the film, as though he and the cold-eyed actor famous for playing villains were outdoing one another in cynicism. By comparison, Chaplin's work beside fat Billy Gilbert (as Herring, the Goering parody) is noisy sound-era slapstick in the tradition of Abbott and Costello and the Three Stooges. More sublime is the casting of Jack Oakie as the jut-jawed Benzino Napoloni, a highly likable Mussolini parody whose upstaging and deflating of Hynkel shows how vulnerable he is and makes it easier to accept the logic of his replacement by the Barber. From Broadway and the Yiddish stage, Chaplin brought

Maurice Moscovich as the dignified, pessimistic Mr. Jaeckel, the strong
paterfamilias to whom the other ghetto dwellers turn for advice and
leadership. Moscovich, who was to die a few months before the film
came out, lends mortal heaviness to the early ghetto scenes, an air of
gloomy fatalism and sour acceptance of oppression as the status quo. His
heavy dignity is an ideal contrast to the lightness of Hannah and the
Barber—and the wonderful silliness of Reginald Gardiner's fruity-
voiced characterization of Schultz, the aristocratic but tolerant Aryan
who befriends the people of the ghetto. An English actor, Gardiner
projected just the right quality of stiff-upper-lip dottiness to make
Schultz decent, human, and funny as the kind of man who brings along
his golf clubs when he escapes the stormtroopers.

Chaplin finished his shooting in March of 1940, only two months
before Hitler's shooting broke out in Western Europe. There were
rumors that Chaplin's new film had been shelved or was being delayed
because of fear that the public was in no mood to laugh at Hitler, but as
the spirits of the British lifted in the first months of the new Churchill
government, there was a sudden rush to release *The Great Dictator*.
When the film went on to become the most financially successful of any
of Chaplin's initial releases,[11] the people who had said that Chaplin was
overstepping himself were confounded. Chaplin, not Hitler, turned out
to be the one who knew what would play in Peoria, Prague, Potsdam,
and Paris.

Given the problems facing him during the creation of *The Great
Dictator*, it is not surprising that Chaplin fell back on *Modern Times* for
countless details, images, gags, and even a specific line: "Actions speak
louder than words." Charlie's lock-step marching in the prison scene is
translated into the Barber's goose-stepping in a concentration camp, the
smut-faced, orphaned Gamine in the dark dress moves bodily from the
slum to the ghetto; Charlie's wide-eyed, faunlike pursuit of one blonde
secretary evolves into Hynkel's snorting as he forces his attentions on
another; Charlie's final gibberish song becomes Hynkel's initial gibberish speech—and *Modern Times*'s opening suggestion that some men
have allowed themselves to become sheep or parts of a huge machine is
echoed in the Barber's closing insistence to his listeners that "you are not
machines, you are not cattle, you are men."

Of all Chaplin's features, none has a simpler, more apparent structure
than *The Great Dictator*. The main story takes place in Tomania between
the two world wars; before and after this main story come scenes of
nearly equal length involving the Barber wearing the uniform of his
country in foreign lands and in different wars: in the plain uniform of a
private in France at the end of the old war, in the equally plain uniform of
the Dictator in Osterlich at the start of the new war. This simple and

orderly structure allows Chaplin to span twenty years, two wars, and the polarities of ghetto and palace, kindness and cruelty, barber and barbarian.

In the "prologue," Chaplin echoes the entire opening sequence of *Modern Times* by introducing the Barber as a humble soldier who is caught up and spit out by the machinery of war. Like Charlie, this conscript will end up in a mental institution. And with good reason: in Chaplin's fifteen-minute summary of the Barber's adventures in World War I, nothing turns out as expected and everything has the taint of nightmare. The sight and situation gags are funny, but they all share common themes to be expanded in the story of Hynkel: that all efforts at destruction will boomerang, that allies and enemies are hard to tell apart. Pulling the lanyard of a huge field gun aimed at a cathedral in Paris, our hero blows up a nearby outhouse; snapping his fingers in annoyance, he tries again and winds up being chased around by the defective shell that oozes out of the muzzle with dreamlike slowness; manning an antiaircraft gun, our hero cannot get it up and threatens his comrades on the ground; trying to throw a hand grenade, he drops it down his sleeve. Only after the first three "boomerang" routines does Chaplin introduce one that is thematically appropriate to the Jewish character: he gets lost in the smoke during an attack and finds himself turned around and on the wrong side—the people he thinks are his countrymen are actually the bloodthirsty enemy, just as later his Aryan countrymen will get lost in a medieval fog and try to kill him.

The fifth and final opening routine (the Barber's upside down flight in Schultz's plane) punctuates the failure of the Tomanian war machine in World War I and brilliantly foreshadows the topsy-turvy reversal on which the film ends: just as Schultz needed the Barber's help at the controls of the plane, he will later force the Barber to take control of the entire Tomanian war machine.

Rarely noticed by Chaplin's critics, never discussed in terms of his narrative function, Schultz is one of the finest and most fully realized of Chaplin's comically human characters. If there is any real hope for the world depicted in *The Great Dictator*, it is in the existence of decently imperfect men like Schultz—men who are imperfect because they are humans, not machines. The only character who bridges the world of the palace and the ghetto until the Barber becomes the master of Tomania's destiny, Schultz is the blessedly weak human link in the chain of dictatorship. Essentially an exhalted courier, a bearer of messages, Schultz enters the story in 1918 with dispatches that might make the difference between victory and defeat for Tomania in World War I—he fails to deliver those dispatches, but at the end of the film, after Tomania launches a new war, it is Schultz who delivers the Barber to the podium and insists that he deliver the speech that will, presumably, save Tomania and the world from Hynkel's tyranny. "You'll speak," Schultz whispers to the Barber. "You must! It's our only hope." The Barber's final speech closes the "contemporary" portion of the film that began when a voice-over narrator told us that, following Tomania's defeat in World War I, "Only the voice of Hynkel was heard." Between the first public address by Hynkel and the speech on which the film ends, it is the perseverance of Schultz that makes it possible for the world to hear the voice of the Barber.

Chaplin's parody of Hitler's speaking style is too famous to need discussion here. Enough to say that, funny as it is, Hynkel's speech is an assault on the senses, an act of aggression toward not only Hynkel's enemies but the audience itself as well as the film industry. "You wanted me to talk," Chaplin seems to be saying, "but if you prefer this talk to the silence of Charlie, you're fools!" That Hynkel is antithetical to silence is summed up in the line ("Things have been quiet in the ghetto, lately") that ends Hynkel's first appearance and allows Chaplin to cut to the ghetto.

Timing the film reveals that Chaplin devotes forty-seven minutes to the scenes involving the noisy Hynkel in his palace or among his cohorts and forty-six to the quieter affairs and concerns of the ghetto: earning a living, making friends, staying alive. The most fully shaped juxtaposition of the polar opposites of palace and ghetto comes just before the middle of the film. In the palace, Hynkel performs a graceful, tender, seductive ballet with a globe of the world, all to the delicate, dreamy prelude to Hitler's favorite Wagnerian opera, *Lohengrin*. The scene is completely expressionistic, for the music comes from no apparent source and the globe is nothing more than a balloon. Most impractical as a piece of office furniture, this balloon is a wonderful objective correlative of Hynkel's fragile dream of possessing the world. When Hynkel's mere touch causes his dreamworld to burst, Chaplin cuts to the ghetto, where the Barber, moving to the frantic rhythm of a Brahms rhapsody issuing from a radio, yanks and scrapes a straight-edged razor over his customer's face without once drawing blood. The difference in touch is the difference between tragedy and comedy, between aspiring toward the ideal and settling for the real. The Great Dictator is left in despair by the bursting of his balloon; the little Barber sticks out his hand for payment and receives it from his startled but relieved customer.

But the Barber and the people of the ghetto are no less subject to folly and dreams than Hynkel and the people of the palace. Hynkel dreams of world dominion, Hannah and the Barber that they can lead normal lives in abnormal times—that they can live in the same world with Hynkel. "Wouldn't it be wonderful if they stopped hating us?" asks Hannah, looking directly at the camera after a stormtrooper is polite to her. "Wouldn't it be wonderful if they let us live and be happy again?" Chaplin answers the question by cutting to the palace, where a henchman comes in to announce that "We've discovered the most wonderful, the most marvellous poison gas. It will kill *every*body!" Back in the ghetto, Hannah and the Barber meet for their first date while their neighbors of all ages look on in happy anticipation. But a minute later, as they stroll arm in arm, their courtship is interrupted as Hynkel's gutteral voice explodes from loudspeakers and the pogrom begins.

The remainder of the film is devoted to the struggles of the people of the ghetto to find the right response to madness. Listening to Hynkel's speech, the Barber at first resolves to stand his ground—and almost immediately nose-dives into a rain barrel. This "fight or flight" syndrome is expanded upon at greater length over the next twenty minutes or so, most fully in the vacillations of Mr. Jaeckel. Learning that the stormtroopers are about to enter his courtyard, he tries to rally his neighbors: "We've got to make a stand. We might as well die as go on living like this." A minute or two later, Jaeckel changes his mind when the Barber insists on taking his advice: "Don't be a fool! You want to be murdered?" In another few minutes, Jaeckel is involved in a plot to blow up the palace—but soon changes his mind again: "We've all been foolish. Our place is at home, looking after our own affairs." Within another few minutes of screen time, he and his family flee their Tomanian home for the false safety of neighboring Osterlich.

The exodus into Osterlich is presented in dreamlike terms: first we see the Barber in a concentration camp as he climbs into his bunk and closes his eyes. Then, as in a dream, we see Hannah and the Jaeckels smiling hopefully as they cross the border. The montage that follows is quite lovely, but such lyrical passages in Chaplin's films (the dream of Heaven in *The Kid*, the dance of the dinner rolls in *The Gold Rush*, the globe-dance in this film) are invariably flights from an unpleasant reality or the result of some kind of social or personal disorder. Thus, we may be moved by the idyllic life Hannah and her relatives lead in exile (Mr. Jaeckel picking grapes happily under the sun and wiping the good sweat from his brow, sun-hatted Hannah running through the flowery fields with dirndl-clad children, the refugees sharing their meals al fresco under the arbor outside their cozy peasant cottage), but even as we read Hannah's letter to the Barber telling him about how happy they are and how they are looking forward to the day when he can join them, we know that it is only a matter of time before the Tomanian army invades Osterlich.

What were the characters to do in the middle of the nightmare? What, for that matter, were the real people trapped in the actual nightmare to do? In mid-1939, shortly before he began filming *The Great Dictator*, Chaplin ordered that receipts from European showings of his new film should be turned over to a Viennese organization that was helping Jews emigrate from Central Europe.[12] By the time the film came out, there was nowhere on the Continent (except, possibly, Switzerland) where it could be shown—and no easy means of escape. Chaplin, too, was trapped by the narrative monster he had created: "It would have been much easier to have the Barber and Hannah disappear over the horizon, off to the promised land against the glorious sunset," Chaplin wrote shortly after the film was released. "But there is no promised land for the oppressed people of the world."[13]

If flight was not the solution, was the answer to fight? If so, how was one to fight and against what or whom? The first part of Chaplin's answer is to be found in the earliest efforts by the Barber and Hannah to resist the stormtroopers. These efforts are ultimately as futile and dangerous as the Barber's efforts at soldiering in the opening sequence, but they give Hannah, initially, a false sense of accomplishment. Dusting off her hands after knocking out a pair of stormtroopers, she tells the Barber, "That did me a lot of good. You sure got nerve, the way you fought back. That's what we should all do—fight back. We can't fight alone, but we can lick 'em together." Though her speech is delivered with considerable gusto and appeal, and though her actions amuse us and provide Chaplin with an opportunity to show his grace when the Barber staggers about like a mechanical doll after being hit on the head with a frying pan, Chaplin is careful to challenge or refute her speech on three points. First, hitting the stormtroopers may have given her some satisfaction, but a minute or so later they return with reinforcements to lynch the Barber—what is good for her is not necessarily good for others. Second, what she sees as courage in the Barber is actually the naively spontaneous reaction of a man who does not know what is at stake—it is no more courageous than Charlie's unknowing flirtation with gravity in *The Gold Rush*. Finally, Chaplin seems to imply that her call for resistance is mistaken on at least two counts: the stormtroopers cannot be overcome even by the collective effort of the ghetto—and they are not the real enemy. Having made these mistakes early in the film, Hannah will reveal her conversion when she foils Schultz's well-intentioned but (in Chaplin's eyes) foolish plot to blow up Hynkel in his palace.

All of the mistakes and indecision of those who oppose Hynkel and what he stands for is avoided by the Barber when he finally steps up to the podium to deliver, as Hynkel, the five-minute long speech on which the film ends. As Chaplin was careful to point out in a press statement, the speech "is addressed to [Hynkel's] soldiers, the very victims of a dictatorship."[14] The Jewish hero has pulled off a trick of Old Testament simplicity and chutzpah: he has entered the camp of the enemy and subverted it to his own purposes. The speech may be taken as a general appeal for brotherhood, but within the context of the Barber's masquerade it is also a direct, practical order to the Tomanian army from its commander in chief.

Though some early critics and reviewers were favorably impressed by the speech ("simple and tritely wordy compared with any of Mr. Churchill's, [it] takes us by surprise and moves us at levels not touched by 'we shall meet them on the beaches'"[15]), the typical response was that the Barber's transformation into a messianic orator was too sudden, too "out of character." Chaplin was unmoved by these complaints: "To me, it is a logical ending to the story. To me, it is the speech that the little barber would have made—even had to make. People have said that he steps out of character. What of it?"[16] Chaplin's "logic" is that of the miracle, for it is in the nature of miracles—and of their universal popular appeal—that they happen to the most unlikely of individuals: the little shepherd boy who slays the giant warrior, the virgin who bears a child, the simple carpenter who frames a new religion. Nothing less than a miracle could get Chaplin and the Barber out of the fix toward which *The Great Dictator* was propelled by the art of Chaplin and the reality of Hitler.

Having amused us with his early mock-Teutonic parody of Hitler, Chaplin ends with an approximation of the mad fervor of Hitler in order to demonstrate the miraculous power that descends on the Barber—and to prove that he is equal to the challenge of the spoken word in all its manifestations from comic to serious. Ironically, it seems to be Chaplin's understanding of Hitler's oratorical powers that so many of his critics object to not only when they complain about the didacticism, contradictions, and bombast of the final speech, but when they say that the Barber is "out of character." In truth, the Barber has taken on the character of Hynkel, just as Chaplin has gotten inside Hitler, who himself seemed to step shockingly out of character so that "a limp, little man changed into a force of overwhelming power, the stream of speech stiffening him 'like a stream of water stiffens a hose.'"[17]

Finally, there were some critics who objected that Chaplin had erred by substituting words for actions at the end of the film. It is, however, to Chaplin's eternal glory that he could find no more appropriate action than saying words that needed to be said, for it is an essential human trait to offer magical incantations, prayers, laws, myths, poems, and narratives as verbal bulwarks against the disorders of man and nature. Part of the major accomplishment of Chaplin in this, his first genuine "talkie," is that when he finally opened his art to the full range of the possibilities of the spoken word, he also opened his mind and heart. He asked himself what words were good for and under what conditions words might—

within his film and within reality—be preferable to actions. He then systematically undercut the hypothesis that "actions speak louder than words" by putting it into the mouth of a crackpot inventor and by having Garbitsch, the propaganda minister, assert that words like "*democracy, liberty,* and *equality* . . . stand in the way of action." Once Garbitsch has said that, it is the duty of the Barber to stand up and speak such forbidden words.

Monsieur Verdoux: "At Your Service"

As he had after finishing the First National contract and *Modern Times,* Chaplin again tried to avoid the question of what new role he would adopt after *The Great Dictator* by busying himself with developing a script for an actress. Estranged from Paulette Goddard and about to be divorced, he became professionally and personally interested in Joan Barry, a handsome but disastrously unstable young woman. Hearing her read from a recent play, *Shadow and Substance,* Chaplin bought the film rights and hired Barry with the intention of building his new film around her in the role of Brigid, who is described as "small, possibly a little stupid-looking, with large eyes. . . . obviously not mentally outstanding, but capable of deep affection, and pleasing in her person"[18]—a description that fits perfectly such Chaplin heroines as Merna, the blind girl, and most of the characters played by Edna Purviance.

Though there is no record of Chaplin's interest in playing the male lead in a film based on *Shadow and Substance,* it seems likely that another reason for his interest in the play was that the central role of the aging priest was a model for all of the starring roles he would undertake in his remaining films. As autocratic and fastidious as Verdoux, Calvero, and King Shahdov, the old priest is the great dictator of his rectory and parish. At the end, the old priest asks himself, "Am I just an embittered old man . . . living here with shades too glorious to forget?" It was a question that Calvero and Chaplin could have asked. The fact that he turned to someone else's material for inspiration is a sign of his difficulties in motivating himself and his next film. Another sign is the fact that he not only agreed to consider playing the lead in a film to be directed by someone else but ended up purchasing the idea and turning it into the script for what would become his next film. That the idea—a comedy based on the career of Henri Landru, a French confidence man guillotined in 1922 for the murder of ten women—came from Orson Welles is significant, for only a few years before, the young Welles had arrived in Hollywood to shoot his first film under conditions of control that only Chaplin enjoyed as star, director, producer, and writer of his own projects. Neither Chaplin nor Welles could have known in 1942 that

Welles's career was about to go into a precipitous and spectacular decline—and that by giving Chaplin the idea for *Monsieur Verdoux*, Welles was contributing to the delinquency of a major.

By late 1942, Chaplin had a punning title that summed up the comic mixture of seduction and murder that had attracted him to Welles's suggestion: "Lady Killer."[19] After working for months on the Bluebeard script, and finding it hard to motivate, he put it aside when an agent introduced him to a seventeen-year-old aspiring actress who seemed ideal for the lead in his abandoned adaptation of *Shadow and Substance*. The girl was Oona O'Neill, the daughter of the playwright Eugene O'Neill. Chaplin tested her for the part, signed her to a contract, married her, learned she really did not want to be a movie star after all, and permanently shelved the story of Brigid. Settling down to begin a second family with Oona in 1943, Chaplin returned to the "Lady Killer" story he would spend the next three and a half years developing and filming.

Despite the happiness of his new marriage and his joy in the birth of the first children borne to him by a woman he loved, these years were among his most troubled. He was sowing the seeds of his eventual political exile by speaking out in favor of helping the Soviet Union in a time of growing anti-Communist fervor in the United States. Old friends and advisors like Henry Bergman and Alf Reeves had died, and another old friend, Konrad Bercovici, was suing him for plagiarizing *The Great Dictator* (after six years of legal footwork, Chaplin settled by paying Bercovici $95,000 to drop his claim). The worst blow came from Joan Barry, who in 1943 announced she was carrying Chaplin's child. Though he was cleared of charges that he had violated the Mann Act by transporting Barry across state lines for immoral purposes and though blood tests proved that Chaplin could not have sired the child, a jury eventually declared him to be the father and he was required to provide financial support.

Perhaps it was the discrepancy between his happy private life with his new family and the lurid publicity that grew out of the efforts of prosecutors to put him in prison for his various "crimes" against Barry and the moral order that gave the final shape to the Bluebeard script: mild-mannered Henri Verdoux would murder or attempt to murder variously miserly, vain, or foolish women in order to provide a secure home for his little boy and his crippled wife, Mona (Oona?). Critical commentary on the autobiographical nature of *Monsieur Verdoux* is unavoidable; unfortunately, it has usually been limited to drawing obvious connections between the courtroom experiences of Chaplin and Verdoux or between Verdoux's supposed antagonism toward women and the accusations of sexual crimes and emotional cruelty brought against Chaplin by Mildred

Harris, Lita Grey, and Joan Barry. Largely unnoticed is the extent to which Henri Verdoux is a gloss on Chaplin the artist rather than Chaplin the man. Clare Sheridan reports that when Chaplin looked at the bust she did of him in 1921, he mused aloud that "'It might be the head of a criminal, mightn't it?' and proceeded to elaborate a theory that criminals and artists are psychologically akin [because] 'both have a flame, a burning flame, of impulse, vision—a side-tracked mind and deep sense of unlawfulness.'"[20] For Chaplin, the exploration of the criminal psychology of Verdoux was equivalent to the exploration of his own methods and motives as an artist.

Chaplin hints at the "professional" similarity between himself and his character through Verdoux's antique shop, which is little more than a studio warehouse or property room where Chaplin displays the castoff residue of his earlier masquerades next to the detritus of Verdoux's. A stout dressmaker's dummy, first glimpsed in the bedroom of one of Verdoux's victims, stands near the graceful nude statue we saw in *A Woman of Paris* and *City Lights.* Subtitled "A Comedy of Murder," *Monsieur Verdoux* is a sampler of gags spanning Chaplin's career in film comedy, which is perhaps why Chaplin devotes more space to this film than to any other in *My Autobiography,* where he calls it "the cleverest and most brilliant film I have yet made" (*A,* 454).

Monsieur Verdoux opens with two scenes that suggest Chaplin was trying to distance himself from his audience by erecting artificial barriers. First, we see Henri Verdoux's gravestone as the gentle, good-natured voice of the occupant tells how he came to be in the business of "liquidating members of the opposite sex" as "a business proposition" to support a home and family. The tone of Verdoux's voice makes it clear he is quite content with his present condition and that he has no remorse for his crimes. By letting us know Verdoux is a self-satisfied, unrepentant murderer who has been in his grave for ten years, Chaplin makes it difficult for the audience to want to get involved or even to wonder how things are going to turn out. No wonder Luis Buñuel, the great surrealist filmmaker who delights in assaulting and insulting the conventional formal, narrative, and moral expectations of his audience, pontificates that "Chaplin deserves all his fame and universal acclaim . . . for two films: *The Gold Rush* and *Monsieur Verdoux.*"[21] Especially Buñuelian is the claustrophobic domestic scene that follows the one in the graveyard. We find ourselves in the dining room of a dreadful provincial family squabbling about the mysterious man who fast-talked a missing relative, Thelma, into marriage. This scene contains so many apparent flaws—stagy acting, an immobile camera, self-conscious dialogue, old-fashioned production values, and obviously middle-American actors who make no effort to seem French—that it becomes impossible to take seriously anything that follows. The scene is so bad that it is good. When, five minutes after the end of the credits, Chaplin finally appears as Verdoux, we see a fussy, fastidious little man tending the garden of his villa in the south of France. His first line is addressed to the spirit of Charlie as much as to the caterpillar he tenderly moves from harm's way: "Ooh, la la—you'll be stepped on, my little fellow, if you're not careful." In the background, the household incinerator belches black smoke. Though it is never established that Thelma is in the smoke, no other conclusion would be likely two years after the world learned what went on in the Nazi concentration camps. The holocaust reference seems intentional: in *The Great Dictator*, Chaplin had cut away from a fire in the ghetto to show Hynkle/Nero at the piano; now, while his latest victim goes up in smoke, Verdoux goes inside and sits at his piano to lose himself in music. Up to this point, Verdoux's first scene has been elegant, controlled, formal. Suddenly something disturbs Verdoux's aesthetic delight, disturbs the ordered perfection of his art: there seems to be an "echo" in the piano. Verdoux plays several notes and listens in consternation to a little wooden rapping or knocking. It turns out to come not from the piano but from the back door: an ugly, dumpy old woman is there—the cleaning lady. And so it will go all through the film: every one of Verdoux's elaborate schemes comes to grief because of a woman.

Looking closely at Verdoux's absurd rationalization for murdering an endless stream of well-off, "useless" women to keep his small family comfortably housed and fed, we see that even Verdoux's beloved wife gets in the way of the perfection of his schemes, for she seems unimpressed by the comfort and affluence he supplies and looks back fondly to the days when they were so poor they had to live in a single room. The point, of course, is that Verdoux's sentimental rationalization is just another part of his imaginary world. With daring disregard for his audience's ability to follow him to the Olympian heights of aesthetic detachment, Chaplin devotes less than ten minutes to scenes involving Verdoux's family (and nearly half the time in those scenes is taken up with Verdoux talking to his dreary friend, the druggist who dabbles in poison). Further, Chaplin's only effort (and a feeble one at that) to create sympathy for the wife comes at the very start of the first scene when Verdoux greets his crippled wife in their country garden—but the garden is not idyllic, the actress who plays the wife projects no inner or outer beauty, and the child is not even cute.

The woman who causes Verdoux the most comic grief is the indestructible Annabella, a figure of incredible vitality and vulgarity played with brilliance by the brassy Martha Raye. Not since his work with Mabel Normand and Marie Dressler in 1914 had Chaplin been teamed with a talented and experienced comedienne. Even today, Martha Raye's half hour of screen time can convulse an audience. And in the handsome, stately Madame Grosnay—a grandly matronly character apparently created with Edna Purviance in mind but played with regal aplomb by Isobel Elsom, a veteran of the British and American stage and film— Chaplin created a second Amazonian antagonist whose very presence in the film prevents us from taking Verdoux seriously as a lady killer. Clearly, these two strong women can look out for themselves. When Verdoux finds himself trapped in another garden with Annabella and Madame Grosnay, his speculation in wives collapses and he flees over the garden wall.

At that point, with the flight from the garden, Chaplin is ready for the ending that lifts the film above farce. First, Chaplin supplies a humorless montage showing the collapse of the stock market in which Verdoux has been investing the profits from his wife-murdering business. Then, as soon as Verdoux learns that he has lost his little home, Chaplin dissolves to a deadly serious montage showing the rise of Fascism and the coming of World War II. *The Great Dictator's* jokes about Hitler and Fascism are wiped out: where we saw fake Tomanian tanks advancing across a fake landscape, where we saw Hynkel and Napoloni, we now see the real thing. As at the end of *The Great Dictator*, the time for laughter is over. It is time to get serious, time to pay the piper—time for the duty dance with death without which no art is possible. When the montage is over, we discover an older, tired Verdoux reading a paper with headlines that tell us about a massacre of innocents in Spain. Dispirited, he is more dark-clad than before, as though in mourning for the world. Getting up, he walks with stooped shoulders and a shuffling gait.

What now follows is equivalent to the end of *The Great Dictator* after the montage showing the Tomanian invasion of Osterlich. The street-walker whose life Verdoux once spared suddenly reappears to do for this film what Commander Schultz did for *The Great Dictator*: to push the Chaplin figure toward the formal delivery of the film's "message." Just as Commander Schultz came back into the Barber's life in a big touring car, the nameless girl played by Marilyn Nash makes her fortuitous reentry in a chauffeur-driven limousine. And just as the Barber had forgotten that he once saved Schultz's life, Verdoux has forgotten his earlier kindness to the girl. And whereas Schultz had allied himself with Hynkel and the Sons of the Double Cross, the girl has become the mistress of a munitions manufacturer. The explosive source of her new wealth star-tles Verdoux, who says "That's the business I should have been in."

His rueful comment seems the first step in the full awakening that is about to hit him in the restaurant scene, where, in a voice that sets the tone of sad dignity and resignation we will hear throughout *Limelight*, Verdoux tells the girl how the death of his little family was followed by his awakening, as from a dream. He looks back on all that amuses us, on his life as a lady killer, as "a numbed confusion, a nightmare in which I lived in a half dream world, a horrible world. And now I have awakened. Sometimes I wonder if that world ever existed." At this point, his awakening is not complete, for he still embraces his despair as "a narcotic—it lulls the mind into indifference." Just as Commander Schultz refused to let the Barber sink into oblivion, the girl now urges him to hang onto life, even if he cannot see the point: "Life is beyond reason; that's why you must go on, even if it's only to fulfill your destiny." Verdoux laughs gently at her optimism, but just then one of the dreary sisters from the first scene walks in and Verdoux suddenly realizes that he does indeed have a destiny.

Though he has an opportunity to escape, Verdoux says good-bye to the girl and, with his first genuine show of confidence since he fled his marriage to Madame Grosnay, tells her that "I'm going to fulfill my destiny." After a graceful, sprightly little "ballet" in which he waits for the police to notice him, he ends the scene by answering a startled detective's "Henri Verdoux?!" with the courteous "At your service." That is not a surrender to despair and oblivion, as most critics seem to think, but a genuine offer from someone who can be of real service.

Verdoux's "destiny" is not death. Rather, it is that of the Barber, to step forward at the right time to deliver a message. It is the destiny of the artist—and like many compulsive artists, Verdoux must pay a high personal price: he gives up his freedom and life for the chance to have the eyes and ears of the courtroom and the press focused on him when he stands up to make his final statement before being sentenced. Thanking the prosecutor for calling him intelligent (and thus "documenting" the intellectual authority of what he is about to say), Verdoux makes no effort to deny his guilt or beg for mercy (just as Chaplin, a master at creating pathos, did nothing to make Verdoux's little family appealing). Instead, he lectures the court patiently, gently. "As for being a mass killer—does not the world encourage it? Is it not building weapons of destruction for the sole purpose of mass killing? Has it not blown unsuspecting women and little children to pieces—and done it *very* scientifically? Heh! As a mass killer, I'm an amateur by comparison." The speech is delivered modestly, effectively. Only at the end, with his sardonic parting shot ("I shall see you all very soon—*very* soon"), does Verdoux indulge in theatrics. In his death cell, he continues the process, lecturing a reporter philosophically: "One murder makes a villain. Millions, a hero. Numbers sanctify." He then gently corrects a priest who wants to help him make his peace with God: "I am at peace with God. My conflict is with man."

Only after he has delivered all of these messages does Verdoux think about himself by accepting a glass of rum and experiencing one last new sensation on the threshold of oblivion. "There is something superb about this moment before death," says Roger Manvell in admiration; something "elemental [as] the loosening of Lear's button."[22] He sighs in contentment and the cell door opens and the light of the rising sun floods across Verdoux, illuminating him from without as the drink warms him from within.

Monsieur Verdoux was so far ahead of its time in style and content—and so unexpected from Chaplin—that contemporary audiences and reviewers were confused and repelled by what they saw or thought they saw. Not that many actually saw the film. Even before Chaplin knew the verdict of the box office, he seems to have known that the press was going to be out for blood. The day after *Monsieur Verdoux* premiered, Chaplin opened a New York press conference with the words, "Proceed with the butchery."[23] When some of the reporters tried to crucify and pillory him with questions about his political beliefs and his personal life, Chaplin tried to answer them with the same aplomb as Verdoux, but he was not equal to the task. Though he and his new film had some admirers and supporters (most prominently James Agee, who placed it "high among the great works of the century"),[24] *Monsieur Verdoux* was attacked by many critics, banned in a few cities, picketed or railed against in others. Worse, it was largely ignored by the public and soon withdrawn from circulation. *A Woman of Paris* had done poorly at the box office as well, but that was largely because his fans wanted to see Chaplin, not a Chaplin film. Now, apparently, the public did not want to see either. Thirty-three years after his film career began in a sudden burst of glory, it seemed to be over.

The Elegant Melancholy of *Limelight*

In 1948, the year after *Monsieur Verdoux* was released, Chaplin disappeared from the index to the *New York Times* for the first time in decades. Not even his nomination by a group of French critics for the Nobel Peace Prize was deemed worthy of note by the national paper of record. A year later he was back in the news, primarily because a United States senator was urging his deportation as an undesirable alien with "Communist" ties. But in 1950, the successful revival of *City Lights* inspired *Life* to report that "A whole generation of moviegoers has been allowed to grow up hardly knowing Charlie Chaplin except as a figure of scandal and controversy."[25] Perhaps as a result of the enthusiasm of new viewers for the strong, sincere pathos of the old story of the tramp and the handicapped girl, Chaplin knew that he was on the right track with the new script he was working on, "Footlights."

It was to be the story of a once great comedian, Calvero (Chaplin, of course), who has lost his ability to be funny and is in danger of drinking himself to death. After saving an emotionally crippled ballerina from suicide and inspiring her to return to the stage, Calvero makes a triumphant comeback and dies in the process. That this is a highly fictionalized commentary on Chaplin's own career is made clear by several small details: Calvero sleeps below a poster identifying him as a "tramp comedian"; in the place of honor above Calvero's mantlepiece is the same formal portrait of young Charles Spencer Chaplin that serves as the frontispiece of this book; the story opens in 1914, the year Chaplin began his career in Hollywood. By filtering Calvero's story through the decades since the start of his own film career, Chaplin also comments upon the span of that career.

Isolated in the mansion where he churned out the 750-page script for his new movie (the average script is only a sixth as long), Chaplin must have reminded some Hollywood cynics of the eclipsed movie star who fills her days by writing a monumental script for a comeback that will never happen in *Sunset Boulevard,* a movie released while Chaplin prepared to reopen his studio on that same ominously named boulevard. There were, of course, huge differences between Gloria Swanson's Norma Desmond and Chaplin, who, surrounded by a growing family, was not a deluded has-been cut off from life, youth, and reality. And while Norma Desmond does an imitation of Chaplin as Charlie and plays bridge with Buster Keaton, Chaplin had better things to do with his time than to imitate himself—and better things than card games for Keaton, who shares the screen with Chaplin and the stage with Calvero in the film's final comic routine.

Although he did not begin writing the script that would become *Limelight* until mid-1949, Chaplin seems to have been working toward that last great film for nearly thirty years. We can find early traces of *Limelight* in *City Lights* (Charlie's efforts to cure the blind girl and save the millionaire from suicide become a single thrust against despair in *Limelight*) and even earlier traces in the story of the dying clown that evolved into *The Circus*. And from *The Circus* itself comes the first hint of the tyrannical side of Calvero, who reminds us of Merna's cruel stepfather in the way he treats Terry: just as Chaplin's circus ringmaster alter ego strikes the tutu-clad, ballet-slippered Merna because she failed to jump through a hoop, Calvero plays the tyrant by striking the identically costumed Terry when she refuses to go on stage. Merna and Terry both choose to stay with the Chaplin persona, who in each case relinquishes the girl to a handsome young man who is a more suitable match.

Other traces of *Limelight* can be found in a story Alistair Cooke told in 1939 of Chaplin's interest in making a short film based on the old French legend of the tumbler who dies in his efforts to honor the statue of the

Virgin by performing a stunt so difficult that it breaks his back (Calvero dies after tumbling from the stage at the end of his final act) and in a story Chaplin's oldest son dated back to 1940 or 1941: it was to be about "a perennial drunk who comes across a little chorus girl who doesn't know he exists, but with whom, in his loneliness, he falls in love."[26]

Ultimately, *Limelight* can be traced back to Chaplin's memories. Like Chaplin's own drunken, failed father, Calvero is given a benefit (but unlike the elder Chaplin, Calvero is able to perform). Terry, the dark-haired, pale ballerina, seems a composite of the three most important women in Chaplin's life: Hetty Kelly (another dark little dancer), Oona (a young woman who could love an old comedian), and his mother (when Terry loses her ability to dance and her will to live, Calvero does for her what Chaplin could not do for his mother when she lost her voice and her mind—he saves her, protects her, and gets her back on her feet with the help of a doctor played by another of Hannah's children).

A close reading of *My Autobiography* reveals so many apparent sources for *Limelight* that one begins to wonder if the process of reshaping his memories for *Limelight* did not affect his feelings about those memories when he came to write about his youth nearly fifteen years later. The rapturous effect of street musicians playing a harmonium and clarinet, the suicidal melancholy of famous English comedians, his mother's malnourishment, the mixed kindness and cruelty of landladies in shabby dwellings, his faulty memory of the name of an impresario (Postant rather than Postance), all found their way into both *Limelight* and *My Autobiography*.

If Chaplin's memories went into *Limelight*, so did much of Chaplin himself. Not only did he write the script and music, choreograph the ballet, design the costumes and makeup, play the lead, direct, produce, and edit the film, but he also sired five members of the cast. We see his three oldest children by Oona in the opening scene; Charles Chaplin, Jr., his older son by Lita Grey, plays a clown opposite Chaplin in the "Death of Columbine" ballet; and Sydney, his younger son by Lita, plays Neville, the young American composer who tries to woo Terry away from Calvero.

In developing the narrative for his new film, Chaplin did what he had so often done before: he borrowed heavily from the film he had just released. This borrowing and reworking, which adds to the almost seamless quality of Chaplin's American features, results not from laziness or a lack of imagination but from the perfectionist's desire to keep refining characters, incidents, and details until their full potential has been extracted. Thus, in the new film he plays a drunken, has-been music hall performer who has reached the same stage in his life and career as Verdoux after the collapse of his matrimonial schemes. "I love women, but I don't admire them," says Verdoux; "I love them," says Calvero of his audience, "but I don't admire them." Verdoux's crippled wife and the beautiful young streetwalker flow together to form the emotionally crippled ballerina Calvero mistakenly believes is a prostitute; the streetwalker and the ballerina both get into trouble for committing petty crimes in order to help men they care for—and are both spared from death by the Chaplin figure; both Verdoux and Calvero must continue their careers under assumed names and both go willingly to their deaths in order to reach their last and greatest audiences.

The greatest similarity between the two films, and the one that would prove most distressing even to Chaplin's admirers, is that Verdoux and Calvero seem to talk too much. But much of Calvero's talk is so hypnotic and lovely that when it is taken in combination with the many repetitions of and variations upon actions, situations, and images, the effect is, in André Bazin's term, "a relaxing of attention" that leaves the mind free to wander and encourages "daydreaming about the images."[27] Thus, the overall effect of Calvero's talk is to return us to an approximation of the personal silence for which Chaplin was famous until *The Great Dictator*. *Limelight* opens like a silent film with an accretion of intertitles and with a series of dreamlike dissolves that take us closer and closer to the image of the dying Terry. First comes the old-fashioned, grammatically incomplete epigraph: "The glamour of limelight, from which age must pass as youth enters." Chaplin next dissolves to a simple and pointedly unfinished statement of narrative content ("A story of a ballerina and a clown. . ."), then to an equally simple statement of the time and place ("London; a late afternoon in the summer of 1914. . ."). That last intertitle dissolves into an elaborate London street scene in which young Geraldine and Michael Chaplin "dance" toward a hurdy-gurdy. Having established the source of the old-fashioned music, Chaplin pans to the front door of the building where Terry and Calvero live as strangers to one another. After moving the camera toward the door, he dissolves through the door into the hall, then moves his camera toward the door of the room where Terry is trying to end her young life and dissolves through that door to the terrible and beautiful image of Terry in her white gown, stretched out against white sheets, an empty medicine vial clutched in one hand.

The image of the dying Terry is the primary visual key to the moral and aesthetic structure of the film. The image itself is beautiful, Chaplin seems to be saying, but it is improper and an abomination that the image must be purchased at the price of the girl's life. Chaplin's self-imposed task was to transform that beautiful but improper image into one that is both beautiful and proper. With typical generosity, Chaplin shows us two ways that image can be made acceptable: as the product of art or age.

In the middle of the film, he transforms Terry's death wish into art by showing Terry in a very similar deathbed pose in a ballet entitled "The Death of Columbine." The intentional similarity between the attempted suicide of Terry and Terry's make-believe death on stage is stressed not only through graphic design but through the casting: Chaplin's half-brother, Wheeler Dryden, plays both the doctor who helps Calvero restore Terry to health and the clown who helps the clown played by Calvero entertain the dying Columbine. Likewise, the death of Calvero at the very end mirrors the suicide attempt of Terry through several formal parallels, the strongest of which is that Calvero dies stretched out on a couch in a pose resembling that of the dying Terry at the start and of Terry as the dying Columbine in the middle of the film.

At the very end of *Monsieur Verdoux*, Chaplin had attempted to recapture some of the power and pathos of his silent films by having Verdoux walk away from the camera toward his death after taking a drink of rum. At the start of *Limelight*, he reappears as a drunk who staggers toward us, thus asserting in very formal terms the immortality of his persona. By entering the last of his American films as a drunk, Chaplin makes a nostalgic return to the tipsy role that led to his first film contract. And by demonstrating once again his ability to create laughter through the pantomime for which he gained fame on stage and screen, Chaplin also asserts the immortality of his silent craft—for Calvero's first scene is as fine a piece of silent comedy as anything in Chaplin's career. After establishing that silence is necessary by gently shushing the children who speak to him, Calvero enters the hallway of the house where Terry is dying and prepares to light a cigar, not knowing (as does the audience) that the hallway is filling up with gas. Because Calvero never smokes in any other scene, the cigar exists only for the anticipation of a slapstick explosion. But before he can strike the match, Calvero smells something disagreeable. First he sniffs his cigar, then he lifts one foot to see if he has stepped in something. The scatological shoe-sniffing gag takes us back to 1916, when, in *The Count*, Charlie notices a foul smell, checks his shoe, and finally discoveres an offensive cheese. There, the gag was merely vulgar; here, it is symbolic of the foul wind that issues from the bowels of the underworld, from death's kingdom.

Whereas Chaplin had dissolved through Terry's door in order to introduce the audience to the girl, Calvero breaks it down and carries her away to his rooms where he restores her desire to live. The total vulnerability of Terry—far greater than that of Merna or the blind girl and unequaled except by that of the Kid—is a wonderful narrative strategy, allowing the sixty-two-year-old Chaplin to play opposite the twenty-one-year-old Claire Bloom, a British stage actress who seems to represent the ideal of fragile beauty toward which Chaplin had been moving all through his career. Terry Ambrose (the last name suggests

Ambrosia, the food that bestowed immortality on the gods) is given a
new life by Calvero and then inspires the once-great clown to return to
the stage for a final performance before the kind of elite audience
Chaplin liked to gather around him for benefit screenings.

The plot is the purest show business hokum, and yet—despite Walter
Kerr's assertion that "there is nothing in *Limelight* which might not have
been written for the stage"[28]—it is perhaps more consciously "cinematic" than anything else Chaplin had ever done. The series of dissolves
through closed doors that take us from the public street to the privacy of
Terry's death chamber; the dissolves that take us in and out of Calvero's
dreams; the use of the same piece of film at the start of both Calvero's
dream about performing the "Animal Trainer Act" and his actual stage
performance of that act; the use of privileged camera angles and close-
ups that would be impossible on the stage (the gag about the mysteri-
ously shrinking leg in the final stage routine, for instance, relies on the
two-dimensionality of film and on the fixed angle of the camera and
would not be as effective on the stage); the overhead shot of the scene-
changing; the trick cut that allows Chaplin and Buster Keaton to walk
behind a screen and come out a second later in new costumes; the many
matched cuts; the identical zooms toward Calvero's audience to connect
a dream and an actual performance; the lyrical use of the moving
camera—these and other devices call attention to how carefully Chaplin
has conceptualized and constructed *Limelight* as a film and for the
camera. Consider Calvero's final comic routine: swept up in his fiddling,
he moves out of the tight frame at the end of one shot—and falls off stage
and out of the frame at the end of the next. By violating the conventions
of the two modes of performance (on stage and before the camera).
Calvero and Chaplin each exploit the comic potentials of their craft.
Contrary to Kerr's claim, there is nothing in *Limelight* that works on any
terms but those of the cinema.

And for the only time in his career, with the exception of *The Face on
the Barroom Floor* in 1914, Chaplin uses flashbacks, incorporating them
into the narrative flow so smoothly that John McCabe mistakenly places
Terry's job in the music store after her recovery from the suicide attempt
rather than in the form of the flashbacks in which she remembers
meeting Neville, the handsome young composer.[29] The flashbacks make
it possible for Chaplin to show Terry as she sees herself: as an idealistic,
shy, and romantic young woman who "sacrifices" herself for the impoverished Neville by giving him extra music sheets and extra change.
"I hardly knew the man," she admits; "it was something I built up in my
own mind."

The story of Neville is a variation on the stories of Terry and Calvero:
illness, the loss of ability to work (his piano was taken away by creditors),
and, eventually, a triumphant performance on the stage of the Empire,

the very same stage where Terry becomes a prima ballerina and where
Calvero reaches apotheosis in his last great performance. Echoing the
introduction of Neville into the narrative in flashbacks, Chaplin has
Calvero "flash" forward by the power of his romantic imagination:
Calvero tells Terry she will meet Neville again and how they will confess
their love to one another. With that prediction, all dreams and
flashbacks end and the remainder of the film is devoted to working out
Calvero's dreams and his predictions about Terry and Neville—or to
commenting upon the relative truth or falsity of those dreams and
predictions.

"In the elegant melancholy of twilight, as the candles flutter. . . he
will tell you that he loves you—and you will tell him you have always
loved him," Calvero predicts at the end of his fairy-tale about how
Neville and Terry will meet again after she has become a famous
ballerina. The reality is less elegant, more melancholy: Terry rises to
fame in Neville's ballet, but the composer's confession of love comes not
at twilight but in the middle of the night; not, as Calvero predicts, on a
summer night beside the Thames but on a cold stoop outside Terry's
shabby lodgings. And she will not be ready to return his love then nor
will we see or hear her return it later—for Chaplin knows enough not to
make all predictions come true within the range of the camera or the
scope of the film. Besides, because Neville, (whose music Chaplin
composed) is an artistic projection of Chaplin himself as well as a
romantic surrogate for Calvero, Terry's repeated claim that she loves
Calvero seems to be a displacement of her love for Neville. Chaplin
supplies one formal hint of this displacement in the scene in which
Calvero and Terry stroll beside the Thames following Terry's recovery of
the use of her legs: when Terry speaks of their future together, she is
simply mimicking, albeit palely by the chilly light of dawn, Calvero's
romantic evocation of a warm twilight.

Calvero's dreams have no higher quotient of literal accuracy than his
predictions. Or, to put it more precisely, just as the "twilight" prediction
came to pass in distorted terms (the wrong season, the wrong time of
day, the wrong man), Calvero's dreams are exactly the opposite of the
eventual reality. When he dreams of performing his flea-trainer act on
the stage of the Empire, the dream ends in the nightmare of an empty
house; in reality he performs the act to a packed and enthusiastic house.
And while Calvero dreams that Terry joins him as a dancing girl in his
comic act on the Empire stage, in reality he becomes a comic-relief
clown in the ballet in which she stars on that stage.

Once Calvero and Terry have put aside their dreams and memories (to
the extent that Chaplin does not incorporate them into the visible
portion of the narrative), the clown who is no longer funny and the

ballerina who cannot even walk get down to the serious business of healing one another. This process is developed and explored through parallel or linked episodes—or individual scenes in which the two problems move side by side toward the linked resolution first revealed in Calvero's last dream, the one about dancing with Terry on the stage as an audience applauds the end of a successful comic routine. Awake, he tells her about the dream and makes her laugh through his gentle mockery of her despair, then talks about his own failure as a comedian, and how his failure drove him to drink, and how drink almost killed him six months before. His optimism about his own situation is intended to cheer up Terry, but when a telegram suddenly arrives with the staggering news that his theatrical agent wants to see him, Calvero reaps an unexpected harvest of pride and enthusiasm. That is, the presence of the girl, together with his desire to inspire confidence in her, combine to benefit Calvero at a cucial moment. And in terms of the romantic formula, the telegram itself is a token that Terry has brought good luck to Calvero.

Though his visit to his agent's office leaves him depressed (he is kept waiting, the job is at a third-rate theater, he can no longer make demands about terms or the way he is billed, and the agent thinks it would be a good idea for him to work under another name), he is still under obligation to help the girl get back on her feet. Speaking to her forcefully about the power of "life, life, life, life," he echoes the "love, love, love, love!" refrain of one of his dream songs. His speech ends on a note of tired resignation as he says good night and the scene fades out, but a fade-in to another day reveals Calvero and Terry dancing, she in her night gown. Spinning around, he lets her go, forcing her to stagger toward him. She laughs in terror—but she laughs. A dissolve shows them dancing again, with Terry now wearing the street clothes that signal her eventual return to the world outside Calvero's room. Another fade-out and fade-in reveals that Terry is able to get around the room by holding on to the furniture. Within a minute or so of the start of his new scene, we learn that Terry is doing all of the housekeeping and cooking for their little domestic establishment and that Calvero is not only starting to believe the things he has been telling her but that he has not taken a drink since they met—that he has, in effect, stopped trying to kill himself with his own brand of poison. As soon as she responds that he is excruciatingly funny without the help of his alcoholic crutch, we hear the postman deliver the letter informing Calvero that he is soon to open at the Middlesex Theater. In spite of his exterior show of confidence, Calvero lies to Terry about the letter, for he does not want her present for his return to the stage. That lie, of course, warns us that his belief in himself and the things he has been telling her is far from complete.

Fading out on the lie, Chaplin fades in on Calvero finishing his "Sardine" song at the Middlesex. When he begins his comic patter, the audience starts to walk out on him—and Calvero aborts his act and quits the stage. Alone in the dressing room, he takes off his wig, mustache, and makeup, something we have never seen Chaplin or his characters do before. This unmasking is clearly a foreshadowing of his death, for at the very end of the film a doctor will, without any clear medical reason, order the removal of the dying Calvero's makeup.

Back in his rooms, Calvero tells Terry of his failure ("It's no use, I'm finished") and begins to weep. Outraged by his weakness, Terry stands up to lecture him and suddenly realizes that she has regained the use of her legs. "Calvero, look, I'm walking." She repeats the news again and again with hysterical, joyous, almost religious fervor. The words "I'm walking" become an incantation—or an operatic refrain as the music rises and a dissolve takes us to the Thames Embankment where they walk together. "Look, the dawn is breaking," she says, calling attention to another simple event that has miraculous, epiphanic meaning for her. But now their emotional states are reversed: Terry is full of hope and optimism, Calvero sunk in gloom.

With the fade-out beside the Thames ends the first of the film's two major parts. Just as the first "act" is set almost entirely in Calvero's rooms, most of the second "act" takes place on stage and behind the scenes at the Empire Theater (in the first part of the film, Chaplin carries us away to three "stage" sequences; in the second part, he returns us to Calvero's rooms exactly three times). The opening of the second part clearly mirrors the opening of the first: instead of the gaiety of the street outside Calvero's building, we have the gaiety of the promenaders and audience on the Empire's mezzanine during a performance. And just as the sound of the street musicians seduced Calvero into his first dream of performance on the stage of the Empire, we are reintroduced to Calvero's rooms by similar music as Terry returns to find Calvero, drunk for the first time since they met, playing his violin in the company of the same street musicians. Acting like Calvero at the start, Terry lectures Calvero on his health; acting like the Terry we first knew, Calvero tells her his career is over and rejects the good news she brings—that he is to play a clown in a ballet at the Empire. His words sound like a rejection of life itself: "I'm through clowning. Life isn't a gag anymore. I can't see the joke."

But Calvero takes the job in the ballet, after all, and we find ourselves in the middle of Chaplin's most complex structural variation, the two-act ballet that recapitulates the two parts of the film itself. In the ballet, the first act takes place in a London garret where Columbine dies in bed, the second in the graveyard where her spirit rises to dance. Within the larger, two part structure of *Limelight*, the first act echoes the scenes in the rooming house while the second act is modeled on the triumphant returns of Terry and Calvero to the stage after they have both nearly died physically as well as professionally. Thus, when Calvero slaps Terry to force her onto the stage for the second act of the ballet, he is reprising, in physical and visual terms, the many verbal slaps he administered all through the first half of the film.

Although Calvero says that he cannot see the joke in "life" anymore, and though he cocks a disapproving brow when he learns that he is expected to be funny in Columbine's death scene, Chaplin knows what the joke is: that the drunken Calvero had been very funny at the start of the movie while Terry was dying in her gas-filled room—and that he will be even funnier at the very end when his desire to get laughs results in such exertion that his heart is fatally strained.

The death of Calvero is Chaplin's last great "effect." Stretched out on a couch, he tells the silent Terry of their future together, touring the world, "you doing ballet, and me comedy." Immediately, he looks up at Neville and repeats the earlier prediction that "in the elegant melancholy of twilight, he will tell you that he loves you." As he speaks, Calvero looks younger, more handsome than ever before. His curly hair is romantically disheveled, his huge eyes dramatically outlined in mascara.

The fact that Calvero knows he is dying does nothing to contradict the essential truth of what he says, the essential truth of all beautiful lies. Earlier, on the morning after Terry's debut as Columbine, Calvero had angrily rejected her proposal that they marry and settle down (shades of Verdoux!) in a little house in the country. He had insisted then that all he wanted was truth in the few years he had left. The stagy, melodramatic delivery of the lines (by Calvero, not by Chaplin) makes it clear that his rejection of Terry is the lie of an old man who knows that the girl is lying to herself when she claims to love him. Terry lies constantly in the name of love or sympathy: she lies about the amount of change Neville is entitled to; she lies when she claims not to love Neville; she even lies when she encourages Calvero to return to the stage, for she rehearses a claque in the belief he cannot succeed on his own. Thus, Calvero's return to the stage is a token of his acceptance of Terry's need to create the beautiful lie on which all of Chaplin's art is based: that the heart will triumph over the mind, life over death, dreams over reality.

Having reached the end of Chaplin's American career, it seems useful to reflect upon two of the most extreme of the negative reactions to *Limelight*—and, by extension, to the social and aesthetic implications of the three films discussed in this chapter, the films Chaplin made after he set aside the persona of Charlie. Because these reactions come from two highly respected critics, and because they have been reprinted and cited, they are touchstones.

First, there is Andrew Sarris's reaction to the self-referential content of *Limelight:* "Ultimately Chaplin lost most of his audience, and in *Limelight* he celebrated the occasion by imagining his own death, a conception of sublime egotism unparalleled in the world cinema. To imagine one's own death, one must imagine the death of the world."[30] But Sarris misses the point. True, Chaplin does imagine the very real possibility of the death of the world in *The Great Dictator* and *Monsieur Verdoux*, but he does so because it is necessary to imagine such a thing in order to speak out against it. If Chaplin does indeed imagine his own death in *Limelight*, it is in the context of Calvero's rejection of Terry's right to take her own life and of his refusal to admit to the finality of his own death. When Calvero tells Terry that they will tour the world together, he is really speaking about the immortality of his own art, for Terry is Calvero's creation in the same sense that *Limelight* is Chaplin's.

Far from being a celebration of the loss of his audience, *Limelight* is a statement of Chaplin's belief that he cannot escape from that audience and the duty to perform. More than twenty years before Calvero came into the light, Thomas Burke wrote that Chaplin "shrinks from the limelight, but he misses it if it isn't turned upon him."[31] The most self-consciously self-referential of Chaplin's films, *Limelight* reveals, in the words of a French critic, "the deep loneliness and uneasiness of every man who has yielded himself up to the public."[32] The Barber, Verdoux, and Calvero are all alike in that they yield themselves up to that public, and in that the yielding takes the form of speech. We must remember that Calvero's last performance ends not with pantomime but with a direct speech to his audience—and that it is followed by his speech to Terry, at whose insistence Calvero returned to the stage. Calvero's last words to Terry are not anticlimactic. They are the climax.

Which brings us to the single most damning indictment of Chaplin's career after he put aside the costume and persona of Charlie and began to speak. In "The Lineage of *Limelight*," a review first published in 1952 and reprinted as the final selection in McCaffrey's *Focus on Chaplin*, Walter Kerr traced what he calls the "hopeless capitulation to words" of *Limelight* back to "the split between the artist and the thinker [that] began with the closing moments of *The Great Dictator*." Kerr's review ends with a scathing attack on "a line of dialogue which summarizes [Chaplin's] whole latter-day development." The offending line is Terry's response to Calvero's insistence that happiness comes from the mind: "To hear you talk," she says, "no one would ever think you're a comedian." Chaplin, says Kerr, knows that the line is a dangerous one. He anticipates its dangers by [having Calvero react] to it with mock dismay, with irony. . . . He secretly hopes that, once he has made light of the whole business, the audience will still be impressed with the things a comedian can say when he puts his mind to it. He wants a disclaimer of intellectuality and an insistence upon intellectuality at one and the same moment. He is conscious of his present course, self-conscious about his present course, and determined upon his present course.

There are wheels within wheels here, but it might have been better had they never been set turning. A profound clown—the greatest, most beloved we have—is seeking a second reputation as a sage. It is not likely to equal his first.[33]

What Walter Kerr seems to want—and it was probably this desire that led him to write his very fine book on the silent clowns—is for the "old" Chaplin to return. In this sense, he is like Terry who cries, "Calvero, come back. You've got to come back." But the Calvero she wants is not the living, breathing Calvero; rather, she wants to possess the Calvero she remembers or imagines. So with Kerr when he refers to Chaplin as "the greatest, most beloved [clown] we have"; those last two words reveal that Kerr believes the audience somehow possesses Chaplin and can summon him back. "Chaplin, come back," Kerr seems to be saying. "You've got to come back." Chaplin could have answered with Calvero's response to Terry: "I can't—I must go forward."

The forward direction Chaplin took in his last three American films was into the increasingly benevolent use of language as a tool for manipulation, seduction, and inspiration of characters within the narrative and of the audiences watching the films. This trilogy began with the words of the Great Dictator leading a whole nation astray until the Barber used other words in an effort to lead the nation back to sanity and decency. Verdoux's early words led women to death, but his later words were directed to bringing the world back to its senses. By the time he made *Limelight*, Chaplin's early dislike for the spoken word had softened to the point that most of Calvero's words are life-giving. While the first two films in this trilogy had ended with benevolent perorations, Calvero's first exchange with Terry is at the same lofty rhetorical level. But notice how carefully Chaplin has undercut and mediated this early rhetoric by making it clear that Calvero is still a bit drunk. "What's your hurry?" Calvero replies when Terry asks him why he did not let her die. "Billions of years it's taken to evolve human consciousness, and you want to wipe it out. Wipe out the miracle of all existence. More important than anything in the whole universe! What can the stars do? Nothing but sit on their axes. And the sun, shooting flames 280,000 miles high. So what? Wasting all its natural resources. Can the sun think? Is it conscious? No, but you are." The big final speeches of the Barber and Verdoux are not funny, but this one is, for the girl has fallen asleep and is snoring in contradiction to Calvero's assertion that she is conscious.

Let there be no mistake about Chaplin's intent in *Limelight*. He was not, as Kerr puts it, "seeking a second reputation as a sage," for the many words spoken by Calvero belong to the character, not to Chaplin. Consider the scene in which the weeping girl complains that Calvero saved her life: sober now, he responds with just the right touch of irony that "Well, we all make mistakes, you know." The gentleness of his delivery, her sudden smile in response to his mockery, the way he sniffs his fingers and then tries to wipe away the smell of kippered herring—of the messiness of life itself—all layer meaning on the verbal content. Far from being a "hopeless capitulation to words," *Limelight* marks Chaplin most hopeful and delicate balancing of the power of words and the beauty of silence.

6

Postmortem Effects

Chaplin in Exile—the Final Films

IN SEPTEMBER of 1952, a month before the release of *Limelight*, Chaplin sailed for Europe with Oona and their four small children. Learning that he would have to answer Immigration Department questions about his political beliefs before he could reenter the United States, he chose to live in Switzerland, where he soon purchased a mansion near Vevey. There he would spend the remainder of his life, a quarter century in which he outlived the controversies that drove him from America, wrote his autobiography, sired four more children, reissued some of his silent films with musical soundtracks, and scripted the two films he made in England in rented studio space.

Though the first of these films, *A King in New York* (1956), was attacked and dismissed as bitterly anti-American, it is a gentle, mellow, and totally innocuous comedy about the misadventures of the elderly King Shahdov (Chaplin) who takes refuge in New York after being deposed by a mob that lynches him in effigy and screams for his head. In Shahdov's first line, delivered as he steps off the plane in New York ("Ha, ha—we fooled them"), Chaplin seems to be jeering at the politicians who drove him from America and at the critics who had announced his professional demise after *Monsieur Verdoux* and *Limelight* were ignored and boycotted. But the line also contains a heavy burden of irony, for Shahdov has only fled from one mob into the embrace of another by coming to America, the land where (in Chaplin's view) the fickle mob is king.

Chaplin and Shahdov are one and the same: clever, resourceful old confidence men who refuse to give up without a struggle. Unfortunately, their struggles are feeble. In spite of their good intentions, Shahdov's nuclear energy scheme and Chaplin's new film were both failures—and for similar reasons: the artist and his persona lacked the technical, economic, and popular resources needed to reach their goals.

Most crucially, their schemes lacked originality and they themselves lacked power and energy. In the film, these inadequacies come together in the fact that Chaplin chose to hide himself behind the persona of a deposed king. Because Chaplin lived like a king and was treated like royalty, there was no metaphorical freshness in his choice; worse, by seeing himself as a king rather than a performer (as in *The Circus* or *Limelight*) or as a projection of the ordinary man, Chaplin built a wall between himself and his audience.

If King Shahdov is a pale shadow of Chaplin, the film itself is a paler shade of his earlier work. Consider the theme of emotional exile that runs through Chaplin's American films from *The Great Dictator* on: the Barber, Verdoux, and Calvero all live in their native lands but have nonetheless been made to feel outcast by racial prejudice, financial disaster, or the relentless onset of age. In *A King in New York*, the exile theme has lost much of its force by becoming literal. Though one might expect an artist self-exiled from America to be able to extract substantial emotional power from the story of an exile seeking a new life in America, Chaplin fails to give us any sense of what Shahdov's lost country means to him. Compounding the failure, Chaplin uses Shahdov's sojourn in America for the most trivial of comic and ironic purposes. True, he does make an attempt to create pathos through the subplot of a ten-year-old American boy who feels a stranger in his own country, but the boy (played by Chaplin's son Michael) is an even paler shadow of Chaplin.

Speaking the film's last line, Shahdov tells the little boy (who has just betrayed his Communist parents' friends to the witch-hunting authorities) that things are going to get better in America and that "there's nothing to worry about." But Shahdov offers no proof and Chaplin does nothing to help us understand or believe that sudden burst of unwarranted optimism. Having abdicated once by projecting his feelings of exile from America onto a child, Chaplin abdicates again by having Shahdov get into a plane and fly back to Europe without having solved any of the specifically American problems raised in the film. The carelessness and lack of direction of the entire film is summed up in the last scene. Chaplin had apparently filmed King Shahdov and his companion seated facing toward the left (or "western") side of the screen. But because the logic of the final scene is that the plane must fly from west to east as it leaves New York, the film had to be printed in reverse so that characters would face to the right. In practical terms, this means no more than that their boutonnieres and handkerchiefs are on the wrong side and that the king is seated in the subordinate position—but the mistake is symptomatic of the many things Chaplin got wrong or backward in *A King in New York*. It was not the kind of mistake Chaplin would have made when his mind was fully engaged by what he was doing—and when he had his faithful crew and company around him at his own studio. Perhaps the greatest single mistake Chaplin made in *A King in New York* (other than the mistake of making it in the first place) was that he misplaced the romantic interest by making the female lead representative of the loud mass culture that he parodies early in the movie, the mass culture of noisy streets and noisier nightclubs and theaters; of teenaged girls rocking and rolling to the beat of a song that insists "If you're not well, take a pill"; of wide-screen movies heavy on sex and heavier on violence. Retreating to his hotel suite, King Shahdov peeps through a bathroom keyhole to discover the girl in the next suite singing in her tub. "I'd sell my soul for love," she sings, and it turns out she will sell anything she can, anyway she can, for she is in advertising. Seduced by her blatantly insincere charms and the sponsors' fees she can get for him, the impoverished king soon becomes involved in the girl's television huckstering schemes. Taking on some of the traits of his adopted country, Shahdov pounces lustfully on his temptress: "This is my revenge," he tells her; hers is to call him "honey" for the rest of the film. At the end, even though King Shahdov is a tremendous success as a television personality (for reasons that are never demonstrated), and even though he has been cleared of Communist ties by a Congressional Committee after he accidentally wets it down with a fire hose, he voluntarily says good-bye to the girl and to America. Andrew Sarris cuts to the tired heart of the film when he suggests that the young woman played by Dawn Addams is a projection of Chaplin's attitude that America is "a fantasy and a delusion, a marvelous world that he may yet revisit but that he will never reconquer."[1]

Another marvelous world that Chaplin could only revisit and never reconquer was that of pantomime. Observe the one scene that seems closest to the old Chaplin, the one in which Shahdov orders caviar and turtle soup from a waiter who cannot hear him over the noise of a loud orchestra. Although it is mildly amusing to watch Shahdov mime both the source of the food and the way it is eaten, the pantomime exists not for its own graceful or comic sake (as does the drunk routine at the start of *Limelight*, for instance), but as a practical means of communication. It is the pantomime of a curmudgeon, of an old man who cannot stand the noise rather than of an ageless, timeless figure who loves silence.

Ultimately, *A King in New York* is like King Shahdov's face-lift: it looks something like the old Chaplin, but the stitches cannot hold up for very long. Touchingly, the comic situation that causes Shahdov to laugh away his new face is an old-fashioned stage routine about paperhanging, the kind of thing Chaplin had done half a century earlier for Karno. But the paperhanging routine is not funny and is not even thematically relevant, for it has nothing to do with the plight of the exiled king or of the benighted America of the McCarthy era. Perhaps the problem was that Chaplin simply was not mad enough, or sufficiently interested, to fight the old dragons of intolerance and cruelty, to fight for the love and attention of the mob. For both Chaplin and Shahdov, exile was to be their permanent state.

A King in New York was greeted with reactions ranging from political hostility to embarrassed attempts not to be too cruel to a fallen artist. A typical testimony of respect came from Kenneth Tynan, who in a review called the film "never boring" but "seldom funny."[2] Even Chaplin admitted to being "disappointed in the picture" and to feeling "a little uneasy about the whole film": "I meant it to be so up-to-date and modern but perhaps I didn't quite understand it. It started out to be very good and then it got complicated and I'm not sure about the end" (ML, 306).

Perhaps taking the universal failure of the film as a sign that it was time to put his career in order, Chaplin began to write his autobiography. Visiting Chaplin while he was at work on the story of his life, Harold Clurman told his readers in Esquire that, "For the first time in my long acquaintance with Chaplin, I had the feeling that he was not only an artist of genius but a man who might be considered—or had become— wise."[3] But reviewing the finished product in the same magazine a few years later, Malcolm Muggeridge would find it "so banal, so tedious, with his name dropping, his taste for exiled royalty . . . , his political and ethical bromides, his arch amours and his everlasting preoccupation with money—that last infirmity of ignoble minds," that he would call it "a truly atrocious book."[4] Published in 1964 under a title made redundant and solipsistic by the personal pronoun, My Autobiography was flawed by huge evasions (the conditions of his second marriage, for instance), careless inaccuracies (according to Chaplin, Fatty Arbuckle survived only a year or two after his infamous arrest and trial; in truth, he lived another twelve years), and ingratitude (Rollie Totheroh and many other important collaborators receive no credit and sometimes no mention). Yet there can be little doubt that Chaplin wrote it himself, for any self-respecting ghostwriter would have at least checked the basic facts, quoted accurately from printed sources, and attempted to impose a clear chronological order. The flaws in My Autobiography, like those in A King in New York, document an artist in the process of dissolution.

With his autobiography out of the way, Chaplin devoted himself to what would, mercifully, be his last film. Based on "White Russian," a script he had written for Paulette Goddard thirty years before, A Countess from Hong Kong (1966) showed that Chaplin was able to adapt to the new demands of wide screen, technicolor, and international star casting. Unfortunately, he adapted so poorly that the film would not be seen today, even as rarely as it is, had not Chaplin made it. Once again he returned to the theme of exile, casting Sophia Loren as "Countess" Natasha, who escapes a Hong Kong dance hall (and prostitution?) by stowing away in the ocean-liner suite of Ogden Mears, an American millionaire played by Marlon Brando, an actor who represents a style of acting totally at odds with the directing style of Chaplin. After excruciatingly dull and pointless efforts to keep her presence a secret, Natasha and Ogden fall in love.

Even today, the old-fashioned qualities of *Limelight* work in its favor because that is the story of a clown who has outlived the prime of his art. To a lesser extent, the stiff, stilted quality of *A King in New York* is appropriate to the dignity of the old king. But there is no mitigating aesthetic justification for *A Countess from Hong Kong* with its mismatched cuts, obvious process shots, illogical plotting, and static camera work—or for the dreary anachronisms of a story that might have been mildly successful had Chaplin made the film when the idea first came to him during the heyday of fluffy studio comedies. The fact that Chaplin did not make "White Russian" in the thirties is a sign of the vitality and originality of the years of his professional maturity; the very fact he made *A Countess from Hong Kong* in the sixties is proof of his dotage.

And yet, the sheer helplessness and vulnerability of Chaplin's last movie has an almost endearing quality, as does Chaplin's final cameo appearance as a seasick (or drunken) steward and the Chaplinesque hat and ill-fitting suit Sophia Loren is forced to wear in memory of Charlie. And when Natasha and Ogden finally lose themselves in one anothers' arms among the dancing figures, we can rejoice that Chaplin had, for the first time since the end of *Modern Times* thirty years before, been able to end a film with a simple vision of happiness. The dance on which the film ends, says one sympathetic critic, "seems entirely appropriate as the final one of Chaplin's career: this gentle little man, having found a fulfilling romance in his own life, communicates the joyous possibilities of love to his audience. And if the audience, and the critics, are too jaded to recognize the profound truth in this scene, it is their loss."[5]

After the release of *A Countess from Hong Kong*, Chaplin talked about other projects to star his many children (a parody of epic movies about "pretentious big things" like the Bible and ancient Rome; a black comedy about a condemned prisoner in Kansas; a fantasy about a girl born with wings), but nothing came of these plans.[6] In 1970, he reissued *The Circus* with a sound track that included an original credit sequence song he croaked himself:

Swing, little girl, swing high to the sky
And don't ever look to the ground.
If you're looking for rainbows, look up to the sky.
You'll never find rainbows if you're looking down.
Life may be dreary, but never the same:
Some days it's sunshine, some days it's rain.

The extreme simplicity of the song, and the fact that Chaplin sang it over images borrowed from the middle of the film, from the scene in which the hungry, tired Merna works out on the trapeze rings, conspired to make it oddly effective and moving. The act of putting a new opening on *The Circus*, minor as it is, marks the end of Chaplin's career as a creator and manipulator of film images.

His last years were a mixture of declining health and the escalating honors that befall an artist who has outlived the passions of his enemies and entered the pantheon of his art. In 1972, he returned to the United States to be honored in New York and Hollywood, where he received a special Academy Award for his contribution to the art of the motion picture. A year later, *Limelight* (which had not had an "official" release under Academy of Motion Picture Arts and Sciences rules when it first came out), won an Oscar for best original dramatic score of 1972. Shortly before his eighty-sixth birthday, he was knighted by Queen Elizabeth II.

Chaplin's last public appearance came in the fall of 1977 when he went to a circus in Vevey and shook hands with a clown. He was eighty-eight. His family seemed to know that the end was near, for they departed from the tradition of including a family picture with their Christmas cards; instead, the photograph that year was of the old man, alone.[7] Sir Charles Spencer Chaplin died in his sleep shortly before dawn on Christmas morning.

The Permanence of Chaplin

In 1932, Chaplin was included in a *New York Times* list of "ten men who stand as symbols of their times": the others were the Prince of Wales, Pope Pius XI, Mussolini, Stalin, Henry Ford, Gandhi, Lindberg, Einstein, and G. B. Shaw.[8] By the time Chaplin died, he had outlived all the rest—and most of them by two or three decades. Were we to make an even more select list today, a list of the ten great figures of this century, most of the other names on that original list might disappear—but Chaplin's would surely remain and would just as surely be the only one to represent the motion pictures. We can be certain of this because of the towering historical figure Chaplin makes as star, director, writer, producer, and subject of his own films. And we can be certain of it because of the human figure he makes, a figure that is both commonplace and heroic, a figure that is still instantly recognizable even to people who have never seen a Chaplin film. The figure that Chaplin makes is independent of his films and of his person. Today, an impersonation of that figure is used to promote the corporate image of IBM, an organization not known for encouraging its employees to emulate Charlie or Chaplin. At the opposite extreme, not even the great wealth Chaplin amassed nor the social and political deviations of Chaplin and his alter egos prevented the official press of the People's Republic of China from eulogizing him for the "deep ideological and social meaning" of his films and for his "profound compassion for oppressed and exploited humanity."[9] Chaplin's reputation, then, has no specific connection to any reality.

So much ink has been spilled in efforts to explain the figure Chaplin makes that it seems unnecessary to spill more here. But let us single out two quotes from among the millions of words by and about Chaplin. First, here is something Chaplin said about himself to a reporter in 1940: "I am protected by being a charlatan. I don't think in terms of common sense and, to be honest, I don't search for truth. I search for effectiveness."[10] What was this effectiveness? André Bazin has come closer than anyone else to exposing the roots of Chaplin's effectiveness:

> Claude Mauriac has rightly pointed out that Chaplin makes the cinema serve him while others make themselves its servant. In other words, he is the artist in the fullest sense of the term, one who meets art on an equal footing. If he expresses himself by way of cinema, it is not so much because his talents and gifts are more readily adapted to it than for example to literature, but because the cinema can express what he has to say more effectively. . . . What is crucial is not Chaplin's objective freedom to choose the cinema but the subjective freedom of his relations with the twentieth-century art par excellence, the film. Chaplin is perhaps the only example to date of a creative person who has totally subordinated the cinema to what he had to say, without worrying about conforming to the specifics of its techniques.[11]

Bazin's final sentence sets the standard against which all challenges to the preeminence of Chaplin must be judged. Has any other filmmaker "totally subordinated the cinema to what he had to say"? Perhaps Ingmar Bergman, Orson Welles, Francois Truffaut, Jean-Luc Godard, Federico Fellini, and a few others have come close in a few films, but always in terms of the times and places in which they worked—and never in the consistently timeless, placeless, private universe Chaplin still occupies. Today, a handful of filmmakers resemble Chaplin in the superficialities of subject matter and approach, but not one brings together the peculiar and particular traits of Chaplin. As director, writer, and star performer, Woody Allen makes himself the center of his own highly personal films, but his persona lacks the universality and timelessness of Chaplin's and his films are rooted in the language and culture of contemporary American life. Robert Altman, whose repertory company sometimes includes Chaplin's look-alike daughter Geraldine, creates very special comic worlds, but without a continuing character. Of all contemporary filmmakers, only Steven Spielberg seems to have the staying power to develop into a creator of comic adventures and fantasies about little men and woman and children who fight and win on their own terms against bullying monsters and bureaucracies—against inexplicably maniacal trucks and sharks, against agencies both governmental and supernatural that seek to take away our lives, our children, or our dreams. But Spielberg does not have the luxury of a single character who can grow like Charlie and still remain forever the same. And Spielberg must often reach outside our world to motivate his plots. Charlie, like Chaplin, was otherworldly, alien, but he was also profoundly human.

Although he left behind a body of work that can be enjoyed and revered for its parts as well as its whole, a body of work that spans the two great eras of film history and is itself great in both eras, Chaplin has influenced no living filmmaker or actor in any way that can be demonstrated except through individual examples of simple imitation and homage. Chaplin became great and remains great because he saw the world as no one else did or could and made films in a way that no one, before or after, could ever hope or even wish to emulate. And that is why there can and will be no more Chaplins.

Notes and References

Preface

1. Jacobs, *The Rise of the American Film* (New York: Harcourt, Brace, 1939), p. 226.
2. Mast, *The Comic Mind* (Indianapolis, 1973), p. 67.
3. Mordaunt Hall, "Shy Charlie Chaplin Opens His Heart," *New York Times*, 9 August 1925, Sec. 4, p. 5.
4. Bercovici, *It's the Gypsy in Me* (New York: Prentice-Hall, 1941), p. 156.
5. Bazin, *What is Cinema?*, vol. 2 (Berkeley, 1971), p. 130.

Chapter One

1. *My Autobiography* (New York, 1964), p. 14; hereafter cited in the text as *A*. Unless otherwise indicated, all biographical information comes from this work, the *New York Times*, or Sobel and Francis (below). Note: all page citations for *My Autobiography* refer to the paperback edition.
2. John McCabe, *Charlie Chaplin* (Garden City, N.Y., 1978), p. 2.
3. Burke, *City of Encounters* (Boston: Little, Brown, 1932), p. 151.
4. *Charlie Chaplin's Own Story* (Indianapolis, 1916), pp. 16–21.
5. Laurel is quoted by McCabe, *Charlie Chaplin*, pp. 27–28.
6. See Plumb's introduction to Roger Manvell, *Chaplin* (Boston, 1974), pp. vi–vii.
7. McCabe, *Charlie Chaplin*, p. 78.
8. This quote, from *The Tatler*, appears in Raoul Sobel and David Francis, *Chaplin: Genesis of a Clown* (London, 1977), p. 9.
9. See *My Autobiography*, p. 187 and *My Life in Pictures* (New York, 1975), p. 112; hereafter cited in the text as *ML*.

Chapter Two

1. Bercovici, "Charlie Chaplin—An Authorized Interview," *Colliers*, 15 August 1925, pp. 5–6.
2. Though *Carmen* was released in four reels, Chaplin intended it as a two-reeler; the extra footage was added by Essanay.

3. Jacobs, *Rise of the American Film*, pp. 237–38.
4. Sobel and Francis, *Chaplin*, p. 72.
5. Gifford, *Chaplin* (Garden City, N.Y., 1974), p. 95.
6. Some prints of *A Day's Pleasure* end with the traffic jam, but in other prints the traffic jam comes before the boat ride, as it does in the list of "titles" Chaplin reproduces in *My Life in Pictures*, p. 183.
7. Quoted from *Classic Film Collector*, in McCabe, *Charlie Chaplin*, p. 108.
8. Harcourt Farmer's prediction is reprinted from the October 1919 issue of *Theater Magazine*, in Stanley Hochman, *A Library of Film Criticism* (New York: Ungar, 1974), p. 44.
9. Eastman, *Sense of Humor* (New York: Charles Scribner's Sons, 1921), p. 120.
10. When Chaplin reissued *The Kid* with a musical score, he reedited it to delete two brief scenes involving the Woman: one in which she contemplates suicide until a toddler distracts her, thus precipitating her decision to retrieve her child from the limousine; another in which she encounters the Kid's father five years later. These changes tend to focus attention on Charlie.
11. *The Plays of J. M. Barrie* (New York: Charles Scribner's Sons, 1928), p. 440; Chaplin admits to being influenced by this play in *My Autobiography*, p. 272.
12. This review is reprinted in *Focus on Chaplin*, ed. Donald W. McCaffrey (Englewood Cliffs, N.J., 1971), p. 106.
13. Burke, *City of Encounters*, p. 172.
14. *My Trip Abroad*, (New York: Harper and Brothers, 1922), p. 8. This book was written with the help of Monta Bell, a former reporter who became one of Chaplin's chief assistants.
15. Sheridan, *Naked Truth* (New York: Harper and Brothers, 1928), p. 274.

Chapter Three

1. Stark Young, "Dear Mr. Chaplin," *New Republic*, 23 August 1922, pp. 358–59.
2. Negri, *Memoirs of a Star* (Garden City, N.Y.: Doubleday, 1970), p. 216. For photographs of Chaplin as Napoleon, see *My Life in Pictures*, pp. 207–10.
3. This story, told by Menjou in *It Took Nine Tailors* (New York: McGraw-Hill, 1948), p. 106, is corroborated by Jim Tully, *A Dozen and One* (Hollywood: Murray & Gee, 1943), p. 32.
4. These dates are given by David Robinson, "*A Woman of Paris*," *Sight and Sound*, Autumn 1980, p. 221.
5. Menjou, *It Took Nine Tailors*, p. 115.
6. Jacobs, *Rise of the American Film*, p. 241.
7. Quoted by Robinson, "*A Woman of Paris*," p. 223.
8. *New York Times*, 7 October 1923, sec. 9, p. 4. The Chicago interview is reported in the *New York Times*, 27 September 1923, p. 10.

9. Richard Meryman, "Chaplin: Ageless Master's Anatomy of Comedy," *Life,* 10 March 1967, p. 94.

10. Kerr, *The Silent Clowns* (New York, 1975), pp. 246–47.

11. Lita Grey Chaplin, *My Life with Chaplin* (New York, 1966), p. 139.

12. Hall, "Shy Charlie Chaplin," p. 5.

13. Kauffmann, "Chaplin's *The Gold Rush,*" *Horizon* 15 (Summer 1973):45.

14. For two eyewitness accounts of Chaplin's interest in playing Christ, see Elinor Glyn, *Romantic Adventurer* (New York: Dutton, 1937), pp. 301–2, and Colleen Moore, *Silent Star* (New York: Doubleday, 1968), pp. 96–97.

15. M. Willson Disher, *Clowns and Pantomimes* (1925; reprint ed., New York: Benjamin Blom, 1968), p. 34.

16. *New York Times,* 16 August 1925, sec. 7, p. 3; 29 November 1925, sec. 8, p. 5.

17. William Dodgson Bowman, *Charlie Chaplin: His Life and Art* (New York: John Day, 1931), p. 122.

18. The divorce complaint in excerpted in Lita Grey Chaplin, *My Life,* pp. 253–55. For more details, see Terry Hickey, "Accusations against Charles Chaplin for Political and Moral Offenses," *Film Comment* 5 (Winter 1969):44–57.

19. Manvell, *Chaplin,* p. 135.

20. L'Estrange Fawcett, reporting in the *New York Times,* 5 September 1926, sec. 7, p. 5.

21. Kerr, *Silent Clowns,* p. 339.

Chapter Four

1. Mast, *Short History of the Movies,* 3d ed. (Indianapolis: Bobbs-Merrill, 1981), p. 229. The "standard" critical approach to Chaplin's resistance to sound is summed up in Ira S. Jaffe's "'Fighting Words': *City Lights, Modern Times,* and *The Great Dictator,*" *Journal of the University Film Association* 31 (Winter 1979):23–32.

2. L'Estrange Fawcett, *Film: Facts and Forecasts* (London, 1927), p. 225.

3. Tino Balio, *United Artists: The Company Built by the Stars* (Madison: University of Wisconsin Press, 1976), p. 91.

4. *New York Times,* 5 March 1930, p. 26.

5. See Theodore Huff, *Charlie Chaplin* (New York, 1972), p. 219; McCabe, *Charlie Chaplin,* p. 170.

6. *New York Times,* 19 November 1925, sec. 8, p. 5.

7. Kerr, *Silent Clowns,* p. 352.

8. Egon Erwin Kisch, "I Work with Charlie Chaplin," *Living Age* (Boston) 337 (15 October 1929):230–35.

9. Eastman, *Heroes I Have Known* (New York: Simon and Schuster, 1942), pp. 178–79.

10. Meryman, "Chaplin," p. 89.

11. May Reeves told all in *Charles Chaplin Intimé* (Paris: Gallimard, 1935).
12. See *New York Times*, 17 March 1935, sec. 8, p. 4.
13. *New York Times*, 5 February 1931, p. 24.
14. These quotes come, in the order given, from Huff, *Charlie Chaplin*, p. 252; Kerr, *Silent Clowns*, p. 354; Gifford, *Chaplin*, p. 107; Manvell, *Chaplin*, p. 140.
15. Cotes first made this error in a review of *My Autobiography* ("The Little Fellow's Self Portrait," *Films and Filming* 11 [December 1964]:12); it has been reprinted in Cotes and Thelma Niklaus, *The Little Fellow* (New York: Citadel Press, 1965), p. 173.
16. A 16mm print of this silent version is in this Kipnis Collection at the University of Florida.
17. *New York Times*, 2 February 1936, sec. 9, p. 5.
18. *Variety*, 11 September 1935, p. 3.
19. Frank, "Funny-Legs," *New Yorker* 1 (23 May 1925):10.
20. Huff, *Charlie Chaplin*, p. 253.

Chapter Five

1. *New York Times*, 15 September 1937, p. 27.
2. *New York Times*, 20 September 1937, p. 22.
3. *New York Times*, 15 April 1932, p. 20.
4. Lillian Ross, *Moments with Chaplin* (New York: Dodd, Mead, 1980), p. 49.
5. Manvell, *Chaplin*, p. 190.
6. Frank, "Charles Chaplin, a Portrait," *Scribner's Magazine* 86 (September 1929):238.
7. Tully, *A Dozen and One*, p. 17; Eastman, *Heroes I Have Known*, p. 161.
8. Waite, *The Psychopathic God: Adolf Hitler* (New York: Basic Books, 1977), pp. 36, 373, 1102, 9, 215, 42.
9. Gerith Von Ulm, *Charlie Chaplin, King of Tragedy* (Caldwell, Idaho: Caxton Printers, 1940), p. 394.
10. *New York Times*, 6 November 1938, sec. 9, p. 5.
11. For the box office success of *The Great Dictator*, see Balio, *United Artists*, p. 164.
12. *New York Times*, 15 June 1939, p. 11; 28 July 1939, p. 6.
13. "Mr. Chaplin Answers His Critics," *New York Times*, 27 October 1940, sec. 10, p. 5.
14. Ibid.
15. William Whitebait, "The Two Charlies," *New Statesman and Nation*, 21 December 1940, p. 650.
16. "Mr. Chaplin Answers his Critics."
17. Waite, *The Psychopathic God*, p. 208.
18. Paul Vincent Carroll, *Shadow and Substance* (New York: Random House, 1937), p. 13.

19. This title is mentioned in the *New York Times*, 16 October 1942, p. 21.
20. Sheridan, *Naked Truth*, p. 271.
21. See Francisco Aranda, *Luis Buñuel: A Critical Biography* (London: Secker and Warburg, 1975), p. 53.
22. In McCaffrey, *Focus on Chaplin*, p. 142.
23. See George Wallach, "Charlie Chaplin's *Monsieur Verdoux* Press Conference," *Film Comment* 5 (Winter 1969):34–43.
24. Agee, "*Monsieur Verdoux*," *The Nation*, 14 June 1947, p. 723.
25. *Life*, 8 May 1950, p. 81.
26. See Alistair Cooke, "Charlie Chaplin," *Atlantic Monthly* 164 (August 1939):185, and Charles Chaplin, Jr., *My Father, Charlie Chaplin* (New York: Random House, 1960), p. 246.
27. Bazin, *What is Cinema?* p. 132.
28. Kerr, "The Lineage of *Limelight*," in *Focus on Chaplin*, ed. McCaffrey, p. 146.
29. See McCabe, *Charlie Chaplin*, p. 219.
30. Sarris, *The American Cinema* (New York: Dutton, 1968), p. 41.
31. Burke, *City of Encounters*, p. 138.
32. J. L. Tallenay, "The Tragic Vision of Charlie Chaplin," *Commonweal*, 6 February 1953, p. 452.
33. In McCaffrey, *Focus on Chaplin*, pp. 145, 147, 148.

Chapter Six

1. Sarris, *The American Cinema*, p. 41.
2. *Observer* (London), 15 September 1957.
3. Clurman, "Oona, Oxford, America and the Book," *Esquire*, November 1962, p. 182.
4. Muggeridge, "Books," *Esquire*, February 1965, p. 54.
5. Michael Kerbel, "*A Countess from Hong Kong*," *Film Comment* 8 (September–October 1972):28.
6. For references to these aborted film projects, see Thomas Quinn Curtis, "Charlie Chaplin at 82," *International Herald Tribune*, 15–16 May 1971; *Variety*, 26 November 1969; Meryman, "Chaplin."
7. See Ross, *Moments with Chaplin*, pp. 61–62.
8. P. W. Wilson, "Ten Men Who Stand as Symbols," *New York Times Magazine*, 10 January 1932, pp. 12–13.
9. Quoted in the *New York Times*, 2 February 1978, p. 24.
10. Robert Van Gelder, "Chaplin Draws a Keen Weapon," *New York Times Magazine*, 8 September 1940, p. 22.
11. Bazin, *What is Cinema?*, p. 137.

Selected Bibliography

Primary Sources

Charlie Chaplin's Own Story. Indianapolis: Bobbs-Merrill, 1916. Withdrawn by
Chaplin shortly after publication, this is a highly romanticized, pseudo-
Dickensian, and obviously ghostwritten account of Chaplin's youth and
hard times. Despite the assertion by Timothy Lyons (see below) that the
only extant copy is in the Library of Congress, many other copies exist.

My Autobiography. New York: Simon & Schuster, 1964. In spite (and sometimes
because) of errors, evasions, and omissions, this book is indispensable to
anyone who wants to know more about Chaplin.

My Life in Pictures. New York: Grosset & Dunlap, 1975. A valuable collection of
photographs, posters, and documents, this volume expands upon *My Autobiography* and is often more revealing about Chaplin's inner life and
feelings.

Secondary Sources

1. Bibliographies

Lyons, Timothy. *Charles Chaplin: A Guide to References and Resources.* Boston: G. K. Hall, 1979. Extremely useful though flawed by errors and
omissions.

Petrie, Graham. "So Much and Yet So Little: A Survey of Books on Chaplin."
Quarterly Review of Film Studies 2 (November 1977):469–83. A helpful
guide to the topic.

2. Books and Articles

Agee, James. *Agee on Film.* Vol. 1. New York: Grosset & Dunlap, 1969. This
volume includes Agee's famous three-part review of *Monsieur Verdoux* (pp.
250–62).

Bazin, Andre. *What Is Cinema?* Vol. 2. Berkeley: University of California Press,
1971. Bazin's essays on *Monsieur Verdoux* and *Limelight* are brilliant and
challenging.

Chaplin, Lita Grey. *My Life with Chaplin.* New York: Bernard Geis
Associates/Grove Press, 1966. Written with or by Morton Cooper, the
second Mrs. Chaplin's memoirs often make Chaplin sound like a cross

between Citizen Kane and the Great Gatsby. On the whole, it seems a plausible portrait of the private Chaplin. The references to the production of *The Gold Rush* are particularly interesting.

Fawcett, L'Estrange. *Films: Facts and Forecasts.* London: Geoffrey Bles, 1927. Contains a useful account (pp. 147–65) of his visit to the Chaplin studio during the filming of *The Circus.*

Gifford, Denis. *Chaplin.* Garden City, N.Y.: Doubleday, 1974. A good brief survey of Chaplin's career; full of unique illustrations.

Huff, Theodore. *Charlie Chaplin.* 1951. Reprint. New York: Arno Press, 1972. Still the best early biography of Chaplin in spite of the fact it was written before *My Autobiography* and relies too heavily on ghost-written material. Huff's memory of what happens in the films is often unreliable, but that is a failing common to all of the biographies listed here.

Kauffmann, Stanley. "Chaplin's *The Gold Rush.*" *Horizon* 15 (Summer 1973):40–47. One of the finest readings of an individual Chaplin film.

Kerr, Walter. *The Silent Clowns.* New York: Knopf, 1975. With Mast (below), the finest critical overview of Chaplin's accomplishment before *The Great Dictator.*

Kisch, Egon Erwin. "I Work with Charlie Chaplin." *Living Age* (Boston) 337 (15 October 1929):230–35. A valuable account of working with Chaplin during the filming of *City Lights.*

McCabe, John. *Charlie Chaplin.* Garden City, N.Y.: Doubleday, 1978. Though his recent biography is very detailed and highly readable, McCabe accepts almost everything without verification and thus repeats factual errors from earlier accounts. He also recounts some implausible details or stories without attribution. He makes so many mistakes about plot details that it is hard to believe he actually looked at some of the films in the course of writing the book—or, if he did, that he was paying adequate attention.

McCaffrey, Donald W., ed. *Focus on Chaplin.* Englewood Cliffs, N.J.: Prentice-Hall, 1971. Useful for its selection of early reviews and commentary on Chaplin, this critical anthology lacks balance in the essays on the later films.

Manvell, Roger. *Chaplin.* Boston: Little, Brown, 1974. Not as flawed as McCabe's biography—but not as detailed. Manvell's critical judgments are usually more reliable than McCabe's.

Mast, Gerald. *The Comic Mind.* Indianapolis: Bobbs-Merrill, 1973. This overview of film comedy contains a fine summary of Chaplin's career and of the ebb and flow of critical reaction to him.

Robinson, David. "*A Woman of Paris.*" *Sight and Sound,* Autumn 1980, pp. 221–23. A model for future Chaplin scholarship, this brief article is based on examination of production records belonging to the Chaplin estate.

Sobel, Raoul, and **Francis, David.** *Chaplin: Genesis of a Clown.* London: Quartet Books, 1977. This very detailed and scholarly account of Chaplin's early career is opinionated, subjective, but thoughtful. It is best for its attention to the influence of Karno and the music hall tradition on Chaplin, weakest in its impatience over Chaplin's human failings.

Filmography

UNLESS otherwise noted, all films listed here were written, produced, and directed by Chaplin. Because so many extremely detailed Chaplin filmographies are already available, only the feature films are given a full listing here. Not included are films like *The Bond* in which Chaplin made brief appearances, the sound versions of Chaplin's silent films, or compilations of short films. Release dates, production information, and reel counts or running times are usually based on Timothy Lyons' *Charles Chaplin: A Guide to References and Resources*. Because silent films were meant to be projected at a slower speed than is required for the projection of films with sound tracks, and because many of Chaplin's early films are available in differently edited versions, accurate running times cannot be supplied for Chaplin's silent films; thus, this filmography gives only the original reel counts for the films before *City Lights*. A handy rule of thumb is that a 35mm. reel would take about ten to twelve minutes to project.

The two major rental distributors of Chaplin's films at the time this volume went to press were Audio Brandon Films (a subsidiary of Films Incorporated) and Blackhawk Films. In addition, most of Chaplin's Mutual, First National, and United Artists comedies can be purchased in the videocassette format from Blackhawk Films. For more information, consult the most recent edition of James L. Limbacher's *Feature Films on 8mm, 16mm, and Videotape* (New York: Bowker). Anyone interested in renting or purchasing Chaplin's Keystone, Essanay, and Mutual comedies should consult page 210 of the Lyons guide cited above for a useful warning about the "accuracy" of the prints.

THE KEYSTONE FILMS
All of Chaplin's Keystone films were produced by Mack Sennett and most were written and directed by Chaplin after *Caught in a Cabaret*.
MAKING A LIVING (2 February 1914; 1 reel)
KID AUTO RACES AT VENICE (7 February 1914; ½ reel)
MABEL'S STRANGE PREDICAMENT (9 February 1914; 1 reel)
BETWEEN SHOWERS (28 February 1914; 1 reel)
A FILM JOHNNIE (2 March 1914; 1 reel)
TANGO TANGLES (9 March 1914; 1 reel)
HIS FAVORITE PASTIME (16 March 1914; 1 reel)
CRUEL, CRUEL LOVE (26 March 1914; 1 reel)

154

THE STAR BOARDER (4 April 1914; 1 reel)
MABEL AT THE WHEEL (18 April 1914; 2 reels)
TWENTY MINUTES OF LOVE (20 April 1914; 1 reel)
CAUGHT IN A CABARET (27 April 1914; 2 reels)
CAUGHT IN THE RAIN (4 May 1914; 1 reel)
A BUSY DAY (7 May 1914; ½ reel)
THE FATAL MALLET (1 June 1914; 1 reel)
HER FRIEND THE BANDIT (4 June 1914; 1 reel)
THE KNOCKOUT (11 June 1914; 2 reels)
MABEL'S BUSY DAY (13 June 1914; 1 reel)
MABEL'S MARRIED LIFE (20 June 1914; 1 reel)
LAUGHING GAS (9 July 1914; 1 reel)
THE PROPERTY MAN (1 August 1914; 1 reel)
THE FACE ON THE BARROOM FLOOR (10 August 1914; 1 reel)
RECREATION (13 August 1914; ½ reel)
THE MASQUERADER (27 August 1914; 1 reel)
HIS NEW PROFESSION (31 August 1914; 1 reel)
THE ROUNDERS (7 September 1914; 1 reel)
THE NEW JANITOR (24 September 1914; 1 reel)
THOSE LOVE PANGS (10 October 1914; 1 reel)
DOUGH AND DYNAMITE (26 October 1914; 2 reels)
GENTLEMEN OF NERVE (29 October 1914; 1 reel)
HIS MUSICAL CAREER (7 November 1914; 1 reel)
HIS TRYSTING PLACE (9 November 1914; 2 reels)
TILLIE'S PUNCTURED ROMANCE (14 November 1914; 6 reels)
GETTING ACQUAINTED (5 December 1914; 1 reel)
HIS PREHISTORIC PAST (7 December 1914; 2 reels)

THE ESSANAY FILMS
HIS NEW JOB (1 February 1915; 2 reels)
A NIGHT OUT (15 February 1915; 2 reels)
THE CHAMPION (11 March 1915; 2 reels)
IN THE PARK (18 March 1915; 1 reel)
A JITNEY ELOPEMENT (1 April 1915; 2 reels)
THE TRAMP (11 April 1915; 2 reels)
BY THE SEA (29 April 1915; 2 reels)
WORK (21 June 1915; 2 reels)
A WOMAN (12 July 1915; 2 reels)
THE BANK (16 August 1915; 2 reels)
SHANGHAIED (4 October 1915; 2 reels)
A NIGHT IN THE SHOW (20 November 1915; 2 reels)
CARMEN (18 December 1915; 2 reels—a longer version with footage not
    directed by Chaplin was released as CHARLIE CHAPLIN'S BURLESQUE
    ON CARMEN on 22 April 1916)
POLICE (27 May 1916; 2 reels)
TRIPLE TROUBLE (11 August 1918; 2 reels—an "unauthorized" pastiche of
    footage from WORK, POLICE, and an abandoned Chaplin film)

THE MUTUAL FILMS
THE FLOORWALKER (15 May 1916; 2 reels)
THE FIREMAN (12 June 1916; 2 reels)
THE VAGABOND (10 July 1916; 2 reels)
ONE A.M. (7 August 1916; 2 reels)
THE COUNT (4 September 1916; 2 reels)
THE PAWNSHOP (2 October 1916; 2 reels)
BEHIND THE SCREEN (13 November 1916; 2 reels)
THE RINK (4 December 1916; 2 reels)
EASY STREET (22 January 1917; 2 reels)
THE CURE (16 April 1917; 2 reels)
THE IMMIGRANT (17 June 1917; 2 reels)
THE ADVENTURER (23 October 1917; 2 reels)

THE FIRST NATIONAL FILMS
A DOG'S LIFE (14 April 1918; 3 reels)
SHOULDER ARMS (20 October 1918; 3 reels)
SUNNYSIDE (15 June 1919; 3 reels)
A DAY'S PLEASURE (7 December 1919; 2 reels)
THE KID (6 February 1921; 6 reels)
Photography: Roland H. Totheroh
Associate Director: Charles Reisner
Cast: Chaplin (the tramp), Edna Purviance (the mother), Jackie Coogan (the kid), Tom Wilson (the cop), Charles Reisner (the bully), Henry Bergman (the flophouse proprietor)
THE IDLE CLASS (25 September 1921; 2 reels)
PAY DAY (2 April 1922; 2 reels)
THE PILGRIM (24 February 1923; 4 reels)

THE UNITED ARTISTS FILMS
A WOMAN OF PARIS (1 October 1923; 8 reels)
Photography: Roland H. Totheroh
Assistant Director: Edward Sutherland
Cast: Edna Purviance (Marie St. Clair), Adolphe Menjou (Pierre Revel), Carl Miller (Jean Millet), Lydia Knott (Jean's mother)
THE GOLD RUSH (16 August 1925; 9 reels)
Photography: Roland H. Totheroh
Associate Directors: Charles Reisner and Henri d'Abbadie d'Arrast
Cast: Chaplin (a lone prospector), Georgia Hale (Georgia), Mack Swain (Big Jim McKay), Tom Murray (Black Larsen), Malcolm Waite (Jack Cameron)
THE CIRCUS (7 January 1928; 7 reels)
Photography: Roland H. Totheroh
Assistant Director: Harry Crocker
Cast: Chaplin (the tramp), Merna Kennedy (the bareback rider), Harry Crocker (Rex), Allan Garcia (the ringmaster), Henry Bergman (the old clown)
CITY LIGHTS (30 January 1931; 87 minutes)
Photography: Roland H. Totheroh
Assistant Directors: Harry Crocker, Henry Bergman, and Albert Austin

Music: Chaplin
Music Director: Alfred Newman
Cast: Chaplin (the tramp), Virginia Cherrill (the blind girl), Harry Myers (the millionaire), Allan Garcia (the butler), Hank Mann (the boxer)
MODERN TIMES (5 February 1936; 85 minutes)
Photography: Roland H. Totheroh and Ira Morgan
Assistant Directors: Carter DeHaven and Henry Bergman
Music: Chaplin
Music Director: Alfred Newman
Cast: Chaplin (the worker), Paulette Goddard (the gamine), Allan Garcia (the factory manger), Henry Bergman (the restaurant owner), Chester Conklin (the mechanic)
THE GREAT DICTATOR (15 October 1940; 126 minutes)
Photography: Roland H. Totheroh and Karl Struss
Assistant Directors: Daniel James, Wheeler Dryden, and Robert Meltzer
Music: Chaplin
Music Director: Meredith Willson
Cast: Chaplin (the Barber and Adenoid Hynkel), Paulette Goddard (Hannah), Jack Oakie (Napaloni), Henry Daniell (Garbitsch), Reginald Gardiner (Schultz), Billy Gilbert (Herring), Maurice Moscovich (Jaeckel)
MONSIEUR VERDOUX (11 April 1947; 122 minutes)
Photography: Roland H. Totheroh, Curt Courant, and Wallace Chewing
Associate Director: Robert Florey
Assistant Directors: Rex Bailey and Wheeler Dryden
Music: Chaplin
Music Director: Rudolph Schrager
Cast: Chaplin (Henri Verdoux), Martha Raye (Annabella Bonheur), Isobel Elsom (Marie Grosnay), Marilyn Nash (the streetwalker), Robert Lewis (Maurice Bottello), Mady Correll (Mona Verdoux)
LIMELIGHT (23 October 1952; 143 minutes)
Photography: Karl Struss
Associate Director: Robert Aldrich
Assistant Producers: Jerome Epstein and Wheeler Dryden
Music: Chaplin
Original Songs: Chaplin and Ray Rasch
Choreography: Chaplin, Andre Eglevsky, and Melissa Hayden
Cast: Chaplin (Calvero), Claire Bloom (Terry), Sydney Chaplin (Neville), Nigel Bruce (Postant), Marjorie Bennett (Mrs. Alsop), Buster Keaton (Calvero's partner)

THE FILMS PRODUCED IN ENGLAND
A KING IN NEW YORK (12 September 1957; 109 minutes)
Production Company: Attica-Archway
Photography: Georges Perinal
Music: Chaplin
Cast: Chaplin (King Shahdov), Oliver Johnston (the King's companion), Michael Chaplin (Rupert), Dawn Addams (Ann Kay)

A COUNTESS FROM HONG KONG (November 1966; 120 minutes)
Production Company: Universal
Producer: Jerome Epstein
Photography: Arthur Ibbetson
Music: Chaplin
Music Director: Lambert Williamson
Cast: Marlon Brando (Ogden Mears), Sophia Loren ("Countess" Natasha),
  Sydney Chaplin (Harvey Crothers), Patrick Cargill (Hudson), Tippi Hedrin
  (Martha Mears)

Index